Nejdet Delener
Editor

Ethical Issues
in International Marketing

Pre-publication
REVIEWS,
COMMENTARIES,
EVALUATIONS . . .

"**E**thical Issues in International Marketing," edited by Nejdet Delener, is a thought-provoking and timely collection of articles. While interest in domestic ethical issues in business and in the societal market concept has been increasing, this book contributes to the field of marketing by explicitly extending the discussion to international business in general, and to developing countries specifically.

Executives, students of international business, and business academicians would all benefit from this special publication.

Trina Larsen, PhD
Associate Professor of Marketing,
Drexel University

"Nejdet Delener's collection of essays, *Ethical Issues in International Marketing*, is a timely and provocative response to a growing concern in international marketing–business ethics in a global environment. As Delener's introduction points out, the field of marketing in general and the subfield of international marketing in particular are frequent targets for charges of unethical behavior. For at least three decades, scholars have investigated whether or not the poor pay more; whether or not advertising practices are deceptive; whether or not advertising unfairly uses gender, age, or racial stereotypes; whether or not marketing research is only thinly disguised promotion, as well as many other critical issues in marketing ethics. Relatively few of these scholars have yet addressed research on international marketing ethics.

This compendium of essays brings together theory development and empirical research and expands the researcher's questions in international marketing ethics. How should we deal with the ethical issues of transnational firms in developing countries? How should we deal with the issue of gray marketing? What theories and conceptual frameworks will help to clarify these issues? Will foreign sales and marketing managers place more weight on moral commitments or action consequences in arriving at ethical decisions? Can foreign consumers' ethical behavior be explained by their ethical orientations?

This collection as a whole provides marketing educators and scholars with a much-needed review of the literature on international marketing ethics. It is a provocative beginning which should stimulate others' work in this evolving field.

Barbara C. Garland, PhD
Professor of Marketing, Clarion University of Pennsylvania

More pre-publication
REVIEWS, COMMENTARIES, EVALUATIONS . . .

"In the past few years, concern over business ethics led to curriculum adjustments at institutions of higher education, but more importantly, businesses themselves took a closer look at the ramifications of unethical and ethical business practices with clients and customers. Now that marketing internationally is beyond the scope of unloading surplus merchandise, the ramifications of ethical and unethical business practices must be observed in light of differing cultures, developing nations and the desire for profit. *Ethical Issues in International Marketing* is an excellent step, not only in educating the reader on the ramifications of ethical vs. unethical decision making by businesses, but also in giving insight on how practitioners might develop new policies and strategies that will assist companies in successfully implementing international ventures that are ethically based.

One article that I found most informative and an important concern to marketers was the paper on international gray marketing. The primary concern is the effect of gray marketing on the image and credibility of the manufacturer, the dealer and the product line. This article focuses on these issues and offers practitioners insight on what leads to gray marketing and how such practices can be curtailed.

This volume is an insightful wealth of information whose timing couldn't have been better. It would greatly benefit practitioners as well as academicians as a source and reference for building new policies, strategies and teachings in ethics in marketing.

Victoria A. Seitz, PhD
Associate Professor, Department of Marketing, California State University at San Bernardino

"**A**s we continue to move into a global economy, an understanding of the theoretical and practical implications of ethical issues becomes imperative. *Ethical Issues in International Marketing* presents a compelling array of articles addressing an area of international marketing that represents an important stream of research in today's complex global environment. This volume also comes as a welcome addition to the existing literature because it provides an interesting collection of some recent conceptual and empirical studies advancing the practitioners' need for information and the academic researcher's desire to advance knowledge. The book begins with Dr. Delener's insightful piece pointing out the dearth of research relating international marketing to ethics.

The first article presents a novel conceptual approach, the social contract perspective, to examine the performance/obligations of TNCs vis-à-vis developing countries. A major contribution of paramount significance to academic researchers is that while conventional wisdom holds that ethnocentric views surface time and again regarding the activities of TNCs abroad, current and future managers need to focus upon the welfare of consumers in developing countries in addition to the profit motive.

The second article on gray markets is an eye-opener, identifying marketing ethical issues pertaining to gray market goods.

The common thread in the next set of empirical studies is the investigation of underlying cultural values in various ethical settings. An interesting departure from previous research is that the study settings are foreign, namely Turkey and Egypt, respectively. The findings provide managers/practitioners valuable insights in ethical decision making in different country settings.

Dr. Pradeep Gopalakrishna
Assistant Professor of Marketing
and International Business,
Hofstra University,
Hempstead, NY 11550

"**T**his is an excellent book for those who care about ethics in international marketing. I am very pleased with this book and the orderliness with which it proceeds. It addresses a wide variety of issues that arise in actual situations that have been rarely discussed in international marketing textbooks. It helps readers not only understand the complicated nature of the topic but also provides them with some empirical studies to develop real-life guidelines in their own affairs.

It is a very practical, informative, interesting, and timely book with real-world experiences and powerful insights. It makes a very significant contribution to our understanding of one of the most neglected areas of international marketing. I strongly believe that it is a "must read" for academicians as well as international marketers.

S. Altan Erdem, PhD
Assistant Professor of Marketing,
University of Houston,
Clear Lake

"**P**rofessor Delener has assembled an important collection of research that addresses the practical and theoretical sides of ethical dilemmas. This needed addition to the literature provides a selection of readings that includes an array of topics vital to the understanding of the complexities of operating in a dynamic international environment overrun with an abundance of ethical challenges. The reader will undoubtedly be more cognizant of the issues at hand and better prepared to examine similar scenarios with a more educated eye. In addition, the study of this information is sure to lead to provocative and in-depth discussions among students and professionals alike.

Sheb True, PhD
Assistant Professor,
Loyola Marymount University,
College of Business

The Haworth Press, Inc.

Ethical Issues
in International Marketing

Ethical Issues in International Marketing

Nejdet Delener, PhD
Editor

International Business Press
An Imprint of
The Haworth Press, Inc.
New York · London

Published by

International Business Press, 10 Alice Street, Binghamton, NY 13904-1580 USA

International Business Press is an imprint of The Haworth Press, Inc., 10 Alice Street, Binghamton, NY 13904-1580.

Ethical Issues in International Marketing has also been published as *Journal of Euromarketing*, Volume 4, Number 2 1995.

The development, preparation, and publication of this work has been undertaken with great care. However, the publisher, employees, editors, and agents of The Haworth Press and all imprints of The Haworth Press, Inc., including The Haworth Medical Press and Pharmaceutical Products Press, are not responsible for any errors contained herein or for consequences that may ensue from use of materials or information contained in this work. Opinions expressed by the author(s) are not necessarily those of The Haworth Press, Inc.

Library of Congress Cataloging-in-Publication Data

Ethical issues in international marketing / Nejdet Delener, editor.
     p. cm.
     Includes bibliographical references and index.
     ISBN 1-56024-735-5 (alk. paper)
     1. Export marketing--Moral and ethical aspects. 2. International business enterprises--Moral and ethical aspects. 3. Consumer behavior–Moral and ethical aspects. I. Delener, Nejdet.
HF1416.E84 1995
174'.4dc20
                                    95-14390
                                        CIP

INDEXING & ABSTRACTING

Contributions to this publication are selectively in-
dexed or abstracted in print, electronic, online, or
CD-ROM version(s) of the reference tools and information services listed below. This list is current as
of the copyright date of this publication. See the end
of this section for additional notes.

- *ABI/INFORM Global* (broad-coverage indexing & abstracting service
  that includes numerous English-language titles outside the USA
  available from University Microfilms International (UMI), 300 North
  Zeeb Road, PO Box 1346, Ann Arbor, MI 48106-1346), UMI Data
  Courier, Attn: Library Services, Box 34660, Louisville, KY 40232

- *ABSCAN, Inc.*, P.O. Box 2384, Monroe, LA 71207-2384

- *American Bibliography of Slavic and East European Studies
  (ABSEES)*, University of Illinois at Urbana-Champaign, 246A
  Library, 1408 West Gregory Drive, Urbana, IL 61801

- *c/o CAB International/CAB ACCESS* . . . available in print, diskettes
  updated weekly, and on INTERNET. Providing full bibliographic
  listings, author affiliation, augmented keyword searching, CAB
  International, Wallingford Oxon OX10 8DE, United Kingdom

- *Cabell's Directory of Publishing Opportunities in Business &
  Economics* (comprehensive & descriptive bibliographic listing with
  editorial criteria and publication production data for selected
  business & economics journals), Cabell Publishing Company, Box
  5428, Tobe Hahn Station, Beaumont, TX 77726-5428

- *Contents Pages in Management*, University of Manchester Business
  School, Booth Street West, Manchester M15 6PB, England

- *Foods Adlibra*, Foods Adlibra Publications, 9000 Plymouth Avenue
  North, Minneapolis, MN 55427

- *GEO Abstracts (GEO Abstracts/GEOBASE)*, Elsevier/ GEO Abstracts,
  Regency House, 34 Duke Street, Norwich NR3 3AP, England

- *Human Resources Abstracts (HRA)*, Sage Publications, Inc., 2455
  Teller Road, Newbury Park, CA 91320

- *Journal of Health Care Marketing "abstracts section,"* Georgia
  Tech-School of Management, Ivan Allen College, 225 North Avenue
  NW, Atlanta, GA 30332

- *Management & Marketing Abstracts*, Pira International, Randalls
  Road, Leatherhead, Surrey KT22 7RU, England

(continued)

- *Operations Research/Management Science*, Executive Sciences Institute, 1005 Mississippi Avenue, Davenport, IA 52803

- *Sage Public Administration Abstracts (SPAA)*, Sage Publications, Inc., 2455 Teller Road, Newbury Park, CA 91320

- *Sage Urban Studies Abstracts (SUSA)*, Sage Publications, Inc., 2455 Teller Road, Newbury Park, CA 91320

- *Social Planning/Policy & Development Abstracts (SOPODA)*, Sociological Abstracts, Inc., P.O. Box 22206, San Diego, CA 92192-0206

- *Sociological Abstracts (SA)*, Sociological Abstracts, Inc., P.O. Box 22206, San Diego, CA 92192-0206

- *World Agricultural Economics & Rural Sociology Abstracts,* CAB Abstracts, CAB International, Wallingford Oxon OX10 8DE, England

SPECIAL BIBLIOGRAPHIC NOTES

related to special journal issues (separates)
and indexing/abstracting

☐ indexing/abstracting services in this list will also cover material in any "separate" that is co-published simultaneously with Haworth's special thematic journal issue or DocuSerial. Indexing/abstracting usually covers material at the article/chapter level.

☐ monographic co-editions are intended for either non-subscribers or libraries which intend to purchase a second copy for their circulating collections.

☐ monographic co-editions are reported to all jobbers/wholesalers/approval plans. The source journal is listed as the "series" to assist the prevention of duplicate purchasing in the same manner utilized for books-in-series.

☐ to facilitate user/access services all indexing/abstracting services are encouraged to utilize the co-indexing entry note indicated at the bottom of the first page of each article/chapter/contribution.

☐ this is intended to assist a library user of any reference tool (whether print, electronic, online, or CD-ROM) to locate the monographic version if the library has purchased this version but not a subscription to the source journal.

☐ individual articles/chapters in any Haworth publication are also available through the Haworth Document Delivery Services (HDDS).

Ethical Issues in International Marketing

CONTENTS

ABOUT THE EDITOR

Nejdet Delener, PhD, is Associate Professor of Marketing at the College of Business Administration, St. John's University, New York. He holds a PhD in Marketing from City University of New York; an MBA in Marketing and Finance from New York University and APC in Strategic Planning from New York University. Dr. Delener has published over sixty papers in major refereed journals including the *Journal of the Academy of Marketing Science, Journal of Advertising Research, The Journal of Consumer Marketing, Journal of Euromarketing, Journal of International Consumer Marketing, Journal of Business Research, The International Journal of Bank Marketing, Journal of Midwest Marketing, Journal of Professional Services Marketing, Research in Marketing* and *Advances in Marketing.*

Dr. Delener has also presented numerous papers at regional, national and international conferences including the American Marketing Association, the Academy of Marketing Science, and the American Institute for Decision Sciences.

Introduction

I am very pleased to offer this special volume on the very important and contemporary topic of Ethical Issues in International Marketing. Dr. Nejdet Delener of St. John's University is to be congratulated for developing such an excellent collection for our readers. All of the manuscripts are very insightful and thought-provoking. These articles will add immensely to the growing body of knowledge in the area.

In his introductory article Dr. Delener identifies major issues involved in international marketing ethics and states that a unifying theme is emerging in this special area.

Questions regarding social responsibility and ethics have always surfaced in discussions pertaining to the operations of transnational corporations in developing countries. Even though there is some understanding about the differing roles of transnational corporations in developing countries, there is little consensus on the specific nature of their functions. Although theorists have offered different perspectives in describing the situation, none seems more promising than the social contract perspective. While focusing on this perspective, the article by Rogers et al. highlights the role of transnational corporations, and their mutual obligations within the sphere of marketing, the nature of products marketed in these countries, and the developing countries' economic welfare.

There is a need to develop and implement a macro-marketing philosophy that incorporates profitability requirements of transnational corporations and the socioeconomic and ecological needs of developing countries. Thus, the foundation of marketing concept

[Haworth co-indexing entry note]: "Introduction." Kaynak, Erdener. Co-published simultaneously in the *Journal of Euromarketing* (International Business Press, an imprint of The Haworth Press, Inc.) Vol. 4, No. 2, 1995, pp. 1-4; and: *Ethical Issues in International Marketing* (ed: Nejdet Delener) International Business Press, an imprint of The Haworth Press, Inc., 1995, pp. 1-4. Multiple copies of this article/chapter may be purchased from The Haworth Document Delivery Center [1-800-3-HAWORTH; 9:00 a.m. - 5:00 p.m. (EST)].

might have to be broadened to include societal concerns. In other words, it is argued that the relationship or the social contract between transnational corporations and developing countries should be built on certain ethical and moral foundations. The relative power and influence that transnational corporations wield in developing countries should bestow upon them a greater sense of duty and responsibility. Responsibilities also stem from the fact that the corporation is made possible by society and society will not knowingly agree to incorporate a firm whose actions do not benefit them. It is this "industrialization by invitation" that forms the basis for the social contract between the productive entity, the transnational corporation, and the society. Since transnational corporations operate only at the behest of the society, the host country has the power to disengage a transnational corporation if it is warranted. To avoid such intervention, it is crucial for transnational corporations to ensure that they act in ways considered to be responsible and moral. When society intervenes to protect itself from the unwarranted influences and actions of transnational corporations, the social contract stands violated. Similarly, developing countries' behavior and expectations need to be conducive to encouraging a lasting social contract relationship.

According to Lynette Knowles Mathur, gray marketing occurs when a firm in the authorized channel sells or diverts the goods to an authorized reseller. Gray markets have annual sales in the billions of dollars, are mostly international, and span numerous and greatly diverse goods. The implications of gray marketing for consumers indicate that the downside, or realized risks, may pose short and long-term costs for them. The significance of the risks may vary depending on whether the consumer willingly assumed the benefits and risks of the gray market good. Also, the consumer may behave unethically if he or she knowingly purchases a gray market good, is dissatisfied, and then complains to the manufacturer or its retailers about problems caused by gray marketing. Stakeholders, including the consumer, should be held responsible for their contributions to gray marketing.

The implications for firms indicate that they may be virtually incapable of stopping some gray marketing activities, such as free-riding. Managers may find that they take more of a reactive stance against gray marketing in such areas as marketing research, advertising, and product and brand name. However, firms may be much more capable of reducing the potential for gray marketing by focusing on pricing, channel control, consumer confidence, and guidelines for marketing ethics.

Given the size of gray markets, the certainty that they will always be a part of international business, and their potential implications for consumers and firms, the significance of gray marketing should continue to be examined. Addressing the relationship of marketing ethics to gray marketing may sensitize firms, consumers, and governments to the causes, effects, and implications of gray marketing.

It is becoming more and more important to understand the underlying factors that determine managers' judgements of subordinates' behavior as ethical or unethical. Traditionally, studies of organizational consequences of employees' behavior have assumed that managerial decisions aimed at influencing subordinates' ethical conduct were affected by consequential considerations (utilitarian ethics). However, recent research findings show that the deontological (moral) considerations prevailed over the teleological (consequential) considerations. The study by Vásquez-Párraga and Kara replicates this study in an international setting and expands the analysis to investigate the influence of socialization and cultural values in ethical decision making.

Turkish sales and marketing managers of both large and small size corporations were contacted through a mail survey. Istanbul Chamber of Commerce provided the mailing list and data were collected by pretested questionnaire. Managers received both English and Turkish versions of the questionnaire. The sample comprised all types of industries in both public and private sectors from 17 different cities in Turkey. Eight selling scenarios were used. Each scenario reflected a combination of deontological and teleological conditions.

The findings of the study indicate that Turkish sales and marketing managers use both deontological and teleological evaluations to form their ethical judgements and a course of action. The deontological evaluations had more influence than teleological evaluations in explaining their ethical judgements. Turkish managers' socialization with their parents influenced teleological evaluations. Also, it was found that the cultural preference also significantly interacted with both deontological and teleological evaluations when explaining the outcomes. Thus, the results present a relevant issue for both marketing scholars and practitioners by providing an empirical corroboration and a meaningful extension of a previously formulated theory of marketing ethics.

The global nature of the competitive environment presents unique requirements for managers as they design operational marketing programs and procedures. Special emphasis has been placed on the need to minimize culturally grounded friction between the firm and its internal and external non-domestic publics.

The research by Al-Khatib et al. investigates the relationship between the consumers' ideology or philosophical ethical orientation and probable reactions to the perceived ethical and/or unethical behavior of the firm. This knowledge could provide valuable input into the decision making process as managers attempt to minimize the incidence of culturally/ethically based conflict with internal and external publics.

The results of the study indicate that in situations where the activity in question either violates the law or results in the obvious harm of another, the personal ideological frame of the consumer affects their perceptions of the ethical nature of the activity. However, in more ethically ambiguous situations, perceptions of the activity appear to hinge on situational factors rather than personal ethical ideology. Knowledge of consumers' perceptions of ethical behavior could provide managers with valuable insight for the design and administration of the firm's marketing and channel strategies, personnel policies, and corporate image.

Erdener Kaynak

The Growing Importance of Ethical Issues in International Marketing and Their Practical Relevance: An Introduction

Nejdet Delener

As the global awareness of ethical and corporate social responsibility issues is continually increasing, conducting business transactions efficiently and effectively in a mere technocratic sense is no longer sufficient to preserve the acceptability of business persons by society. Ethical and corporate social responsibility considerations must become as much an integral part of the managerial decision making process as marketing, production, financial, legal, and human resource considerations. A step toward better global decision making is to be aware of and acknowledge the clash among different cultures. This acknowledgement is really a process of learning about other cultures without making business or moral judgments based solely on United States customs and mores. The business persons should know the historical, cultural, political, and legal facts about a country, as these facts influence the way the business people think, interact, and do business.

While business ethics has flourished as a field of inquiry for the

Nejdet Delener is Associate Professor of Marketing at the College of Business Administration, St. John's University, Jamaica, NY 11439.

[Haworth co-indexing entry note]: "The Growing Importance of Ethical Issues in International Marketing and Their Practical Relevance: An Introduction." Delener, Nejdet. Co-published simultaneously in the *Journal of Euromarketing* (International Business Press, an imprint of The Haworth Press, Inc.) Vol. 4, No. 2, 1995, pp. 5-9; and: *Ethical Issues in International Marketing* (ed: Nejdet Delener) International Business Press, an imprint of The Haworth Press, Inc., 1995, pp. 5-9. Multiple copies of this article/chapter may be purchased from The Haworth Document Delivery Center [1-800-3-HAWORTH; 9:00 a.m. - 5:00 p.m. (EST)].

5

past decade, its theories and analyses have been heavily oriented toward domestic issues and duck difficult international challenges (Donaldson, 1992). The operations of Multinational Corporations (MNCs) have posed major challenges to governments, development agencies, and analysts of international business. Because ethics belong at the core of managerial decisions and strategies, corporate managers need to know the dominant values of their companies' environment and to acknowledge that ethics is an indispensable part of that inquiry.

Marketing, as a business discipline, is particularly vulnerable to criticism of ethical practices. Sub-disciplines of marketing (i.e., advertising, pricing, personal selling, marketing research, and international marketing) offer extensive opportunities for unethical behavior. Generally, commercialism and marketing activities have not fared well in the view of most ethicists, and it is only in recent times that a more thorough examination of business ethics has occurred (Steiner, 1976). The attempted application of ethical principles, to marketing in particular, has received increasing attention within three decades. Literature reveals that most of the marketing ethics studies involve the use of scenarios as research instruments and relate to the following marketing sub-disciplines: marketing management, market research, advertising, retail and purchasing management, and marketing education.

To date, little research has been conducted in the area of international marketing ethics. In the domain of international business, Fritzsche (1986) suggests that "marketing activities have been central to international trade and thus have been the focus of much of the criticism concerning unethical behavior" (p. 85). This focus may be due, in part, to the general inability of corporations to arbitrate conflicting obligations among several constituencies in an international context (White, 1993). Difficulties in resolving these conflicting obligations are caused by three major factors: (1) given the growing complexity of the ethical issues found in the international marketing environment, the number of disputes among constituencies is likely to increase (Fritzsche, 1986); (2) due to lack of familiarity with foreign business customs and practices, marketers may make poor ethical decisions in international markets as compared to their domestic markets; (3) unlike domestic markets, where federal law and Judaeo-Christian traditions guide decision making, greater disagreement can be found on what standards should be used in solving the ethical conflicts which can arise in international business (Andrews, 1986).

Ethical issues of international marketing have been of great significance in recent years due to publicity and controversy generated from certain international cases (i.e., the infant formula controversy; a variety of cases related to the marketing of drugs in third world countries; the Bhopal disaster; one company authorized $59 million in political contributions to Italian political parties, while a second company paid $4 million to a political party in South Korea, a third company reportedly contributed $450,000 in "gifts" to Saudi generals). Furthermore, ethical issues will emerge in the international arena due to significant changes in the environment (i.e., NAFTA, Europe 1992, air pollution, biotechnology, space, exporting waste). Ideally, and in a more perfect world, there would be no need to discuss the ethics and corporate responsibility, and there would be no crisis! The world is not perfect, however; the complexities of today's increasingly interdependent global business society only magnify these imperfections—indeed, oftentimes to the point of the aforementioned crises.

Despite all this scholarly attention, there appears to be a continuing gap between the concept of marketing ethics and their application by marketing practitioners. Nowhere is that gap more noticeable than in international marketing. Likewise, the topic of international business ethics has received only limited and isolated exposure in all but a few texts on international marketing. In fact, it is not at all difficult to point out international marketing and international business texts that contain very little coverage of the other field. A review of the leading journals, conference proceedings, and citation indexes does not produce more encouraging findings, either.

Given the number and the importance of problems encountered by corporations involved in international marketing and the lack of research into the identification and importance of major ethical issues, the preparation of this special volume is part of the effort to identify the unique importance of ethics and corporate social responsibility in global markets. Specifically, the main objective in developing this collection was to provide a valuable resource for enhancing our knowledge of this interesting and important area of international marketing ethics and corporate social responsibility. Therefore, this collection was conceived to allow researchers the liberty to explore the topic in the context of an environment supportive of the difficulties associated with this type of research. Thus, the scientific standards upheld are rigorous but consistent with the topic area. The articles are as diverse as the title implies they will be, yet a common bond is the growing sensitivity that we all share in these issues, whether we are scholars or practitioners.

The first article by Hudson P. Rogers, Alphonso O. Ogbuehi, and C. M. Kochunny presents a social contract perspective for analyzing and evaluating the activities of transnational corporations in developing countries. Next, Lynette Knowles Mathur examines the relationship of marketing ethics, as a subset of business ethics, to gray markets for consumer goods.

The next two articles deal with Turkey and Egypt. The first, by Arturo Vásquez-Párraga and Ali Kara, reports on a survey of Turkish sales and marketing managers, and examines the role of socialization and the role of culture in shaping moral commitment. The second, by Jamal A. Al-Khatib, Kathryn Dobie, and Scott J. Vitell, investigates the relationship between the consumer's ideology and perceptions of ethical behavior in Egypt.

All manuscripts went through the normal double-blind review process and each was revised at least twice before final acceptance. This volume would not have been published if I had not had the support and collaboration of numerous helpers. First of all, as the Editor of this special publication, I would like to express my sincere appreciation to Dr. Erdener Kaynak, for encouraging me to undertake this venture and providing paramount guidance and substantial support throughout the development process. In addition, I would like to express my profound appreciation to the reviewers for their time, diligence, professionalism, and insightful comments. Although a few chose to remain anonymous, I extend my heartfelt thanks to them for sharing with me their vast knowledge and honest views on international marketing ethics and corporate social responsibility.

REVIEWERS CONTRIBUTING TO THIS VOLUME

Ishmael P. Akaah, Wayne State University
Tansu Barker, Brock University, Canada
S. Altan Erdem, University of Houston-Clear Lake
Sevgin Eroglu, Georgia State University
Barbara Garland, Clarion University of Pennsylvania
Pradeep Gopalakrishna, Hofstra University
Sreedhar Kavil, St. John's University
Trina Larsen, Drexel University
Diana Lawson, University of Maine
James P. Neelankavil, Hofstra University
Richard Plank, Western Michigan University
Zahir A. Quraeshi, Western Michigan University
Gillian Rice, American Graduate School of International Management
Shahid Siddigi, Long Island University
Mary Smith, California State University San Bernardino
Ajay Sukhdial, Oklahoma State University
Humberto Valencia, American Graduate School of International Management
Attila Yaprak, Wayne State University

REFERENCES

Andrews, E. F. (1986). Ethics, Capitalism, and Multinationals. In M. W. Hoffman, A. E. Lange, and D. A. Fedo (Eds.), *Ethics and Multinational Enterprise: Proceedings of the Sixth National Conference on Business Ethics,* University Press of America, Lanham, MD, 107-112.

Donaldson, T. (1992). Can Multinational Stage a Universal Morality Play? *Business & Society Review,* Number 81 (Spring), 51-55.

Fritzsche, D. J. (1986). Ethical Issues in Multinational Marketing. In G. R. Laczniak and E. P. Murphy (Eds.), *Marketing Ethics: Guidelines for Managers,* Lexington Books, Lexington, KY, 85-96.

Steiner, R. L. (1976). The Prejudice Against Marketers. *Journal of Marketing,* Volume 40 (July), 2-9.

White, T. I. (1993). *Business Ethics: A Philosophical Reader.* New York: Macmillan Publishing Company.

Ethics and Transnational Corporations in Developing Countries: A Social Contract Perspective

Hudson P. Rogers
Alphonso O. Ogbuehi
C. M. Kochunny

SUMMARY. The presence of transnational corporations in developing countries is brought about by a social contract between the transnational corporation and the developing country. Because of the size and power of the transnational corporation, obligations arise that go beyond economic and legal rights and duties. This creates a complex situation in which transnational corporations' need for profit maximization may conflict directly with developing countries' need for economic growth and development. How transnational corporations act in such situations involves questions that lie within the realm of ethics and morality. A perspective is presented for thinking about and evaluating the activities of transnational corporations in developing countries.

Hudson P. Rogers is Associate Professor, Department of Marketing, Box 43490, University of Southwestern Louisiana, Lafayette, LA 70504-3490. Alphonso O. Ogbuehi is Associate Professor, Department of Management and Marketing, College of Business Administration, Christopher Newport University, Newport News, VA 23606. C. M. Kochunny is Assistant Professor, Department of Marketing and Transportation, College of Business and Management Studies, University of South Alabama, Mobile, AL 36688.

All correspondence concerning this manuscript should be addressed to the first author.

[Haworth co-indexing entry note]: "Ethics and Transnational Corporations in Developing Countries: A Social Contract Perspective." Rogers, Hudson P., Alphonso O. Ogbuehi, and C. M. Kochunny. Co-published simultaneously in the *Journal of Euromarketing* (International Business Press, an imprint of The Haworth Press, Inc.) Vol. 4, No. 2, 1995, pp. 11-38; and: *Ethical Issues in International Marketing* (ed: Nejdet Delener) International Business Press, an imprint of The Haworth Press, Inc., 1995, pp. 11-38. Multiple copies of this article/chapter may be purchased from The Haworth Document Delivery Center [1-800-3-HAWORTH; 9:00 a.m. - 5:00 p.m. (EST)].

11

INTRODUCTION

The debate over ethics and the social responsibility of transnational corporations (TNCs) has received some attention in recent years (Donaldson, 1985; Hoffman, Lange, and Fedo, 1986). These analyses have been largely descriptive, with the emphasis on TNCs' transgression (for example, Armstrong et al., 1990; Silverman, Lee, and Lydecker, 1982, 1986; Kaikati and Label, 1980). The majority of research in this area of business has been undertaken to enhance awareness and understanding of the ethical and social responsibility issues involved in marketing in industrialized countries (Smith and Quelch, 1991a; White, 1993; Beauchamp and Bowie, 1988). Relatively few researchers have focused on the ethical issues involved in the conduct of TNCs in the emerging sectors of the global economy, namely, the developing countries (Silverman, Lee and Lydecker, 1986, 1982; De George, 1986; Donaldson, 1985). The purpose of this paper is to present a social contract perspective for analyzing and evaluating the activities of TNCs in developing countries. The paper focuses on three key issues. First, in their dealings with developing countries, TNCs may need to consider using a modified view of the marketing concept. Second, the modified view of the marketing concept would lead TNCs to view the social contract perspective as an approach that is more useful for conceiving the relationship between TNCs and developing countries. Third, TNCs have defined roles, obligations and responsibilities to developing countries because of the social contract which exists between the TNC and the developing country. In exploring these issues, the paper establishes a rationale for evaluating the presence and actions of TNCs in developing countries.

TRANSNATIONAL CORPORATIONS AND DEVELOPING COUNTRIES

The term "transnational marketing" conveys the idea of marketing carried on in foreign lands and, in some quarters, it is used interchangeably with the term "international marketing" and "multinational marketing" (Cavusgil and Nevin, 1981). Regardless of which term is preferred, global marketing activities form the cornerstone upon which the viability and profitability of transnational corporations rest. This, coupled with the tendency toward the globalization of today's markets (Levitt, 1983), makes transnational marketing practices a concern of marketers and public policy officials alike. Further, most, if not all, developing countries look to transnational corporations as change agents capable of easing or eradicating the problems of inequality and lack of economic growth.

Research has indicated that global corporate technology, and all that it represents, increases the inequity which exists in developing economies (Barnet and Muller, 1974). Transnationals have a proven effectiveness in generating demands for modern consumer goods even among the very traditional sectors of developing economies. Generally, transnational marketing centers around providing a means whereby firms from the developed economies could be trained to recognize, access and profit from their dealings with foreign economies as markets. While firms from developing countries have entered into transnational marketing, the phenomenon remains mostly in the purview of firms from developed countries (Buller, Kohls and Anderson, 1991; *Fortune* 1988; *Wall Street Journal,* 1989). In a comprehensive review of the literature on international marketing, Cavusgil and Nevin (1981) identified eleven areas of contribution to strategic international marketing management. However, none of the eleven areas were directed to studying the impact of transnational marketing on the foreign country from a macromarketing perspective. That there are not studies aimed at filling this gap in the literature provides partial justification for this paper.

Given the power of TNCs in developing countries, however, there is a need for some ethical or normative criteria for evaluating the relationship between the TNC and developing countries, and for determining acceptable operational practices. It is quite possible that the exchanges between the TNCs and developing countries ought not to be viewed in the same way as the exchanges between TNCs and their home country. The very vulnerability of developing countries calls for a modified view of marketing thought and practice. For example, in the home country, strong laws are often enacted and enforced to monitor the practices of large corporations.

In developing countries, such laws are either non-existent or easily circumvented (Cross and Winslett, 1987; Bull, 1982). Therefore, the actions of TNCs in developing countries ought not to be assessed as they are in developed economies.

THE MARKETING CONCEPT AND TRANSNATIONAL MARKETING IN DEVELOPING COUNTRIES

A modified view of the marketing concept provides a useful perspective for addressing the many ethical concerns of TNCs. The marketing concept has, as its core, the notion that marketers consider the needs and wants of the consumer and try to make a profit by satisfying those needs and wants through an integrated marketing system. That marketing, as a field of study, has embraced the marketing concept implies that this concept should function somewhat as an evaluative criterion that guides the actions of marketers.

The applicability of the marketing concept rests on its ability to meet the needs of three major publics: (1) the individual customer, and the society as the ultimate consumer; (2) the firm; and (3) the area of marketing thought and practice. In this respect, Lazer (1969) asserts that marketing must develop its "sense of community, its societal commitments and obligations." This calls for a more comprehensive approach to the operationalization of the marketing concept. Therefore, there is a need, especially within developing countries, to develop and implement a marketing philosophy which integrates the profitability requirements of TNCs with the social, economic and ecological needs of developing countries and those who live in them.

To argue, as do Milton Friedman (1970, 1962) and John S. Mills (1957), that the sole purpose of business is to make profit and that the "invisible hand" of the market is the ultimate guide to marketers is to lose sight of the fact that there are few countries in the world where the market functions as a truly competitive market. Defenders of the "invisible hand" perspective base their argument on a notion of the "invisible hand" as an ideal against which market systems are measured. However, as a standard, the "invisible hand" is hardly an ideal. Even if it were the case, it is unwise to leave questions of morality to the "invisible hand" of the marketplace. Indeed, Cavanagh (1984) asserts that Friedman's approach to business is especially myopic. Mason (1979) notes that being in business merely for making a profit is no more the purpose of the firm than getting enough to eat is the sole purpose of life. While the profit motive is a requirement for the survival of the firm, its purpose ought to be somewhat broader and more challenging (Cross and Winslett, 1987).

The Johnson and Johnson (J&J) "Imodium" drug case (Scanlan, 1991a) serves to illustrate this point. In a situation that can be compared to the 1982 Tylenol cyanide contamination, the Pakistani subsidiary of the J&J company dragged its feet in removing Imodium, an anti-diarrhea drug, from the market although it was established that the drug paralyzed the intestines of infants and caused their death. It took a British television expose to force the company to agree to stop making Imodium and take decisive action to remove the offending drug from stores in developing countries.

In cases such as this, defenders of the "invisible hand" perspective would argue that market forces have, over time, acted to remove the drug Imodium from the market place, thereby solving the moral dilemma. However, a more fundamental question is whether the "invisible hand" leads to decisions that are sound, just, right and, above all, moral. In this case, as in others, the "invisible hand" perspective leads to a reaction in the marketplace that may, in the long-run, settle the moral question by removing offending products from the marketplace. However, in the short-run, the moral dilemma remains and, to turn Keynes on his head, in the short-run, many people may die. This flaw in the "invisible hand" perspective makes it an indefensible moral ideal when it is extended into the global market arena. The "invisible hand" can hardly be manifested in developing countries where the majority of the population is not well-educated about the workings of a market economy. While rational self-interest, in the form of the free market system, provides many benefits, it also breeds an arrogance in pursuing narrowly defined goals and results in an indifference to consequences. Indeed, any firm that focuses exclusively on profitability will attempt to push some of its costs off on others, thereby creating negative consequences (Cavanagh, 1984). Consequently, there is a need, especially within developing countries, to develop and implement a macromarketing philosophy that incorporates the profitability requirements of TNCs along with the social, economic and ecological needs of developing countries. An evenhanded and just system would require TNCs to establish internal decision procedures to examine the negative consequences of their activities and attempt to evenly apportion those costs among those who use their products and those who profit from their activities.

PARAMETERS OF CONSUMER SOVEREIGNTY IN DEVELOPING COUNTRIES

In developed countries, conditions of freedom to choose assume a reasonable level of consumer knowledge about choices among competing products. However, in many developing countries, neither product information nor choice among competing brands exist to the point where marketing could be based solely on the notion of consumer sovereignty. Bowie (1982) notes that where buyers have perfect or near perfect knowledge of the market, and where products marketed are not complex, the notion of consumer sovereignty and individual freedom may not be an unreasonable view. However, where the average consumer simply lacks the necessary information for the attitude of caveat emptor to make sense, the notion of consumer sovereignty may need to be adapted to provide for a more responsible approach to the marketing effort of TNCs.

While consumer sovereignty has a place in transnational business practice, it is neither a necessary nor sufficient approach to ethical business practice. Transnational marketing decisions in developing countries ought not to be based entirely on consumer preference. Indeed, some distinction between consumer wants and needs may be of importance. Some researchers go so far as to argue that not all consumer preferences should be honored by the market place (Donaldson, 1982). Hence, the notion of consumer sovereignty can hardly be morally defended as being the ultimate criterion for determining what a TNC should or should not do. The consumption system is but a subsystem of the larger socioeconomic system and it is only by looking at the effect of the TNC on the wider system that we can find justification for TNCs' actions in the consumption system.

In its broadest sense, the marketing concept needs to be extended beyond merely satisfying the needs of the end user as the customer, to also satisfying the needs of the economy or society as an aggregate of consumers. A broadened marketing concept will enable a TNC to take steps to minimize the likelihood of producing and marketing products that could have markedly adverse effects on the social, political, economic, and ecological environments of developing countries. In a free market economy, the social responsibility of marketers ought to be defined both in terms of the marketing process and in terms of socially defined outcomes. However, given the less than perfect markets and diminished consumer sovereignty in developing countries, the process for justifying the responsibilities of TNCs requires a more careful balancing of the claims of the market per se, and the imperatives of business ethics.

ETHICS AND TRANSNATIONAL CORPORATIONS IN DEVELOPING COUNTRIES

The ethical claims that must be considered in marketing decisions rest on the view that the relationship between TNCs and developing economies exists as a social contract with ethical and moral foundations. In keeping with this social contract, society expects, at the very least, that the TNC, as a productive organization, enhances the general interest of the society and its citizens (Donaldson, 1982). De George (1986) notes that the social contract between TNCs and developing countries implies that, all things being equal, TNCs should: (1) refrain from knowingly doing direct harm to the developing country; (2) seek to produce more good than harm for the host nation; and (3) by their activity, contribute to the host country's development. In anticipation of alternative views of thinking about this relationship, we will discuss two competing and often cited ethical frameworks and show why they are inadequate for thinking about and understanding the phenomenon of transnational marketing in developing countries.

The general notion of ethics is concerned with "what is right" or moral and "what is wrong" or immoral. Consequently, philosophers are concerned mostly with what "ought to be" rather than with "what is." More importantly, morality of action entails acting because we believe that an act is the right thing to do in and of itself (Velasquez, 1982). TNCs, like individuals, are governed by the laws of the various countries in which they operate. While these laws purport to outline and govern the various rights and responsibilities of TNCs, the laws of the various countries may be in conflict with each other. However, unlike individuals, corporations are perceived, rightly or wrongly, to have different and greater obligations than do individuals. Because of their size, power, influence, and role in society, we generally tend to expect and, in some situations, demand more of corporations operating in our society than we do of individuals. Power, influence, and the roles which corporations occupy in society bestow more and greater responsibilities upon them, much akin to the increased and greater responsibilities placed on doctors, lawyers, nurses, and teachers (Sethi, 1975).

However, the literature is full of documented tales of the ills of TNCs operating abroad (De George, 1986; Velasquez, 1982). Several theoretical approaches have been put forward to guide the activities of TNCs in developing countries: relativist theories, utilitarian theories, and social contract theories. An analysis of each viewpoint will show the shortcomings of the relativist and utilitarian approaches and provide reasons for TNCs to adopt a social contract approach to their operations in developing countries.

Figure 1 presents a set of decision rules that TNCs might use, under the relativist and the utilitarian view, when facing an ethical decision in developing countries. Ethical relativists argue that TNCs need to adapt and apply the moral standards of the developing country in which they are operating or risk being guilty of becoming moral imperialists. From this perspective, it is argued that TNCs do not have to follow the moral codes of their home country as long as they are not bound by law to do so; that is, they ascribe to ethical relativism: "when in Rome do as the Romans do." Bowie (1990) asserts that adherence to the relativist perspective is inconsistent with moral language usage and may lead to rather bizarre results.

The relativist argument is often manifested in cases involving bribe payments to officials in developing countries in order to obtain market access or lucrative contracts. In such instances, officers of TNCs generally claim that they are only acting in keeping with local business practices. Even when such disbursements are in

FIGURE 1. Ethical Decision Making Framework.

Situation	Ethical Approach	Decision Rules	+ ives/ – ives
	RELATIVIST (What's ethical is determined by the host culture)	- Does action respect local customs? - Does action follow advice and judgement of nationals?	+ Respect for local customs + Use judgement of nationals in developing country – Can result in personally unacceptable results – Can lead to very different if not questionable actions in different countries – No basis for criticizing what goes on in a host country as long as it follows the customs of that country.
		[IF ANSWERS = YES the act is ethical]	
Marketing Situation in Developing Country (LDC)	**UTILITARIAN** (What is ethical depends upon the outcome which provides the greatest good for the greatest number)	- Does action lead to efficient use of resources? - Do benefits outweigh the costs/harm, i.e., produces greatest good? - Does action account for all stakeholders? - Does action minimize pain suffered by anyone?	+ Relatively easy to use – Desirable ends may result from unjust means – What if the action becomes policy? – Subverts individual rights if overall good is large enough – How are costs/benefits measured? + Forces thinking about general welfare – Does not classify actions as good/bad, i.e., allows personal decision making – Ignores inherently wrong actions if justifiable based on "payoff"
		[IF ANSWERS = YES the act is ethical]	

violation of home or host country laws, some TNCs seek to justify it by claiming that they are merely following the functioning system in the host country. However, such an approach is difficult to defend if only because it assumes that developed countries are the ones that make bribery illegal and that bribery is morally acceptable to many people who live in developing countries. That a certain action is routine is hardly ground to assert that it is morally acceptable (Beauchamp and Bowie, 1988). Bogan (1979) notes that bribery is

prohibited in practically all countries. Thus, while ethical considerations require TNCs to respect the differences in local cultures, the
respected practices need not be those of the most corrupt level of
society (De George, 1990). Noting that some values are universal
and apply without exception, Donaldson and Werhane (1988) reject
ethical relativism because it results in the conclusion that one cannot justify any value judgement whatsoever.

Utilitarians, on the other hand, believe that an act is right if it
produces, or tends to produce, the greatest good for the greatest
number of people affected by the action . . . otherwise the act is
morally wrong. From this perspective, the marketing actions of
TNCs are deemed to be justified if they increase utility, that is, if they
produce greater good for those affected by the strategy than alternative strategies would provide. Adoption of the utilitarian perspective
requires that all those affected by the marketing actions be considered, and that long range effects be considered as well as short range
effects. Thus, if managers of TNCs argue that the payment of bribes
is justifiable on the grounds that the contracts obtained by virtue of
paying a bribe will provide workers with jobs and thus provide
benefits for their dependents, their communities, and the stockhold-
ers of the corporation, their utilitarian calculations may fall short in
not considering the effects of supporting this practice on the long-
term distribution of wealth and incentives to work throughout the
society. Utilitarian calculations can also be based on what satisfies
the preferences of the consumers as expressed in their market
choices when, as noted above, in developing countries the consumers
are not sovereign and their market choices are greatly constrained.
Nor are these market choices, influenced as they are by the marketing strategy of the TNCs, necessarily reflective of the consumers'
needs as opposed to their wants.

Here the argument is not so much against the utilitarian viewpoint as it is against the way this perspective can be used to arrive at
decisions which, in the long-run, serve a disutility by disrupting the
economic and marketing system within a developing economy.
Indeed, such utilitarian-based arguments are really cost-benefit
analyses that may only provide short range or immediate benefits to
the corporation. Therefore, as a perspective for guiding and evaluat-

ing the actions of TNCs, the utilitarian approach may be open to such selfish interpretations.

Because these two approaches accord little or no attention to critical issues such as rights, duties, and justice, they do not provide an adequate foundation for training marketers to make informed ethical decisions in situations involving developing countries. Further, both perspectives focus mainly on the business activity or the micro aspects of the environment in the developing country and ignore the wider macro aspects of the ethical situation. Given the apparent inadequacies of both the relativist and utilitarian viewpoints, the social contract perspective is offered as a viable alternative to guide the behavior of TNCs in developing countries.

SOCIAL CONTRACT THEORY

Productive organizations cannot be viewed as isolated entities unconstrained by the demands of society (Donaldson, 1989, 1982; Keeley, 1988). Indeed, the reason for their existence lies in their capacity to satisfy certain societal interest. The society provides the legal, social and marketing structures within which the productive entity, the TNC, operates and, in return, expects certain benefits for the society from the business activities of the TNC. To the extent that it harms society, business is in violation of the unwritten "macro" social contract which authorizes and enforces profit-taking in exchange for social benefits (Fasching, 1981). For example, society offers private enterprise the legal benefit of being viewed as a separate entity, thereby insulating owners from potential liability and possibly ensuring the success of the enterprise. Once society accords the firm some of the same rights as human beings, it is reasonable to expect the firm to have some corresponding ethical obligations to society (Cross and Winslett, 1987).

The focus in this section is to set forth a framework for conceptualizing the evaluation of the ethical behavior of TNCs operating in developing countries. This framework may be viewed as a schema for assessing ethical behavior. The major focus is on the essential attributes needed to develop a foundation for assessing ethical behavior. The framework presented in Figure 2 shows the factors that influence the making of the social contract between the TNC and the developing country.

FIGURE 2. A Framework of the Social Contract Between the Transnational Corporation and Developing Countries.

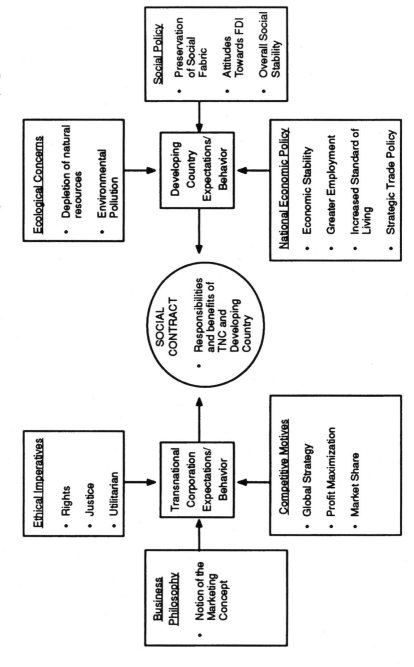

Accordingly, the social contract can be viewed as a joint manifestation of the expectations and behavior of the transnational corporation and the host developing country. Under the social contract there are certain provisions, defined as general minimums, that must be met. Indeed, a number of authors (Dunfee, 1991; Donaldson, 1989, 1982; De George, 1990, 1986; Keeley, 1988) have outlined the kinds of provisions that will make up minimum conditions of the social contract. Beyond these established minimums, contracting parties can enter into a host of arrangements.

In coming together to make the macro social contract the TNC and the developing country are conditioned by a number of different factors and may have vastly different expectations. The nature of the transnational firm's expectations and actions under the social contract is conditioned by three factors: (1) ethical imperatives, (2) business philosophy, and (3) management competitive strategy.

The expectations and behavior of the developing country and its populace, on the other hand, is conditioned more by social policy, national economic policy, ecological concerns, and individual concerns. National economic policy may be driven by the desire for the developing country to devise a strategic international trade policy aimed at establishing economic stability. This can come about through the creation of additional employment with increased foreign direct investments by TNCs. Higher employment and the resulting increase in standard of living will therefore be a major consideration in reaching any social contract with the TNC. Indeed, the need for societal well-being in the developing country may influence the relationship. The country's interaction with the TNC might necessitate laws designed to preserve the social and cultural fabric in the face of social change that might result from the interaction.

These two divergent and oft competing perspectives come together and are sorted out in the social contract. Of basic concern therefore is what general principles, if any, should be in the social contract. What should be the basic terms and conditions of the social contract between TNCs and developing countries? In a broad sense, the social contract defines the rights, duties and responsibilities of both the TNC and the developing country. Therefore, any assessment of the ethics of an act must, by necessity, be conducted with reference to the rights, duties, and responsibilities of the parties as defined in the social contract established when the parties agreed to the relationship. Thus viewed, it is possible to focus on the individual actions, or lack of action, of the parties to the contract and also, it is possible to investigate the ethics of the contract itself. Here, the central idea involves the manipulation of moral variables in the context of a thought experiment designed to ensure procedural fairness in setting the terms of the contract (Donaldson and Dunfee, 1994).

The social contract provides a groundwork for spelling out the macro-level duties of TNCs in foreign markets. Micro-level activities (interactions with customers) should be compatible with macro level norms, By demanding that TNCs honor rights, enhance welfare of workers and consumers at the micro level, and minimize the drawbacks associated with productive organizations, the social contract addresses the question of why a TNC should be moral. Namely, TNCs should be moral because the terms of the contract between the society and the corporation demand that the corporation honor rights as a condition of its justified existence (Donaldson and Dunfee, 1994; Donaldson, 1989; Keeley, 1988).

The social contract helps to organize and stimulate thinking about the role of TNCs in developing countries. In separating ethical arguments from arguments about individual acts, the social contract facilitates the inclusion of macro or societal and micro or individual concerns. Within the context of the social contract, the development of macro ethical analysis facilitates micro analysis by eliminating the need to reference the macro arguments each time a decision is made (Robin, 1992). If TNCs are to become more ethical in their operations, then there is a need to clearly determine what it means to be ethical, both in individual and in organizational activities. This translates into two streams of analysis labeled macro and micro perspectives (Robin, 1992). Accordingly, if they are to effectively predict and eliminate unethical practices, TNCs must be able to describe and understand the global or societal impact of their actions, as well as explain the individual ethical decision making process.

The macro perspective sets the framework within which the individual or micro ethical concerns are examined. The ethical theories used to address macro concerns should provide directions and boundaries for addressing micro concerns. A potential problem arises with this approach because the theories of moral philosophy were designed to direct individual behavior (Robin, 1992). TNCs have constraints placed on them that go beyond those placed on individuals. As such, the social contract theory appears well suited to understanding and assessing the activities of corporations. Indeed, Donaldson and Dunfee (1994) assert that macrocontractors (the TNC and the developing country) are governed by a set of principles (hypernorms) that are so fundamental to human existence that they serve as a guide in evaluating micro-social contract norms (actions involving individuals).

Thus, the notion of a social contract provides a useful framework for thinking about, understanding, and evaluating the actions and social responsibility of both TNCs and developing countries. Indeed, it engages the organization, and/or the society, in a thought experiment that will utilize reason and intuition consistent with achieving moral insight and clarifies the moral basis of organizations. The "social contract" is an attempt to achieve the necessary social activities and associations required, in a civilized society, without giving up or losing basic individual rights. From the perspective of the society, the notion of a "social contract" purports that firms were not based on divinely ordained hierarchies extending from God through governments to corporate managers (Boatright, 1993). Firms were the result of agreements between men, "social contract," in which men surrendered some freedoms to protect their natural rights to the pursuit of life, liberty, and property. However, liberties once surrendered were not forever lost. No corporation has a right to survival at any cost, and firms that violate natural rights and oppress the disadvantaged deserve to be put out of business (Fasching, 1981). Indeed, business has a minimum ethical responsibility to comply with laws which seek to encode natural rights (Cross and Winslett, 1987).

The social contract framework seeks to establish obligations to the developing country that are over and above the TNCs' need to maximize short-term consumer utility and corporate profit. The social contract, while unwritten, is viewed as a moral ideal against which political and business actions can be evaluated. The framework is realistic, however, in that beyond providing goods, services and growth potential, the social contract recognizes the need for TNCs to profit from their operations in developing countries.

In developing countries, the size and power of TNCs give rise to greater responsibilities. Because of the social conditions in many developing countries, there is some justification for holding TNCs to higher moral standards (Laczniak and Naor, 1985; Gough, 1957). On the basis of these higher moral standards, TNCs have both negative duties (to refrain from doing certain things), and positive duties (concrete productive duties to bring about action) in developing countries. Morris (1985) notes that, at a minimum, business should obey the law, which is justified by the need to promote the common good and which may even be essential to the functioning of the free enterprise system. Because TNCs tend to play a dominant role in the economy of most developing countries in which they operate, there is a need for establishing the social contract as a basis for assuring both the rights and obligations of the TNC. For the developing country, the protection of rights and the determination of TNCs' obligations is critically important because TNCs often exercise power equal to or exceeding that held by the government of the developing country because of the vast amount of resources and international connections at the disposal of the TNC (Cross and Winslett, 1987).

The presence of a TNC in a developing country is a direct result of an implicit or explicit social contract between the developing country as the host country and the TNC as a welcomed guest. This social contract is made by the officials of the developing country on behalf of its citizens and is predicated upon the belief that economic growth and modernization will be facilitated through a relatively high level of interaction with TNCs. It is this "industrialization by invitation" that forms the basis for the social contract which exists between the TNC and the developing country. This implied social contract imposes obligations upon both parties–upon the host country and upon the TNC. Generally, the aim of host countries is to provide investment incentives in return for employment, import substitution, exports and overall economic improvement.

Donaldson (1989, 1982) notes that, in return for the right to operate as a business, individual members of the society expect to benefit in terms of enhanced satisfaction of their economic interest to include improved efficiency, higher levels of output and product distribution, income and employment benefits. These prima facie benefits constitute a set of reasons why a society would justify allowing a TNC to operate in the host country. The social contract framework seeks to balance these benefits against the many drawbacks arising out of corporate activity. Indeed, society also expects to minimize the drawbacks associated with pollution and depletion of resources, destruction of personal accountability, and misuse of power. On balance, the social contract recognizes that there are tradeoffs between the needs of the society and the TNC. However, the tradeoffs between the two sides are such that both expect the benefits to outweigh the drawbacks of enacting the contract.

Under the social contract, TNCs are able to operate only at the behest of the society in the host country. In theory, therefore, a society has the power to disengage and even to expel a TNC if it is warranted (Boatright, 1993). When the host country has a relatively powerful government, it is crucial for TNCs to act in ways that are morally responsible to avoid such intervention. When economic realities make it impossible for some developing countries to disengage from the contract, TNCs still have an obligation to be morally responsible. The social contract framework suggests that TNCs must take into account the interest of the host country and its citizens. In this respect, TNCs must recognize that, apart from satisfying their own needs, they also exist to satisfy the needs of the host country and its citizens.

THE SOCIAL CONTRACT
AS A DECISION-MAKING FRAMEWORK

This section seeks to illustrate how TNCs can make use of the social contract framework to guide their business activities in developing countries. The social contract view, as the basis for international marketing decision-making, is a complex macro/micro perspective that requires careful analysis. This macro/micro dichotomy suggests that the business interactions between TNCs and developing countries should be viewed in terms of their implications for both the individual consumer and the society as an aggregate. The macromarketing perspective refers to a level of business activity at which TNCs envisage the economy of the developing country as an ultimate consumer whose needs must be addressed. Indeed, the broad-based societal needs must be satisfied even as TNCs seek to address needs and wants at micro level, usually individuals or organizations as consumers. Figure 3 presents a set of decision rules that managers might adopt in determining the ethics of an action.

While the model is aimed at analyzing business interactions at the macro level, it can also be applied at the level of interactions with the individual consumer. However, the problem with the micro approach to the needs satisfaction in developing countries lies in the fact that the TNCs conceive of the consumer as being sovereign. Hence, they generally end up adopting a marketing strategy that satisfies individual consumer need for foreign products (micro perspective) without respect to the effect of such practices upon the economy of the developing country (macro perspective).

For example, in the "Infant Formula" case, as in many of the cases involving the exportation of drugs and pesticides, the TNC was seen as overly concerned with market share and profits. This emphasis led to a reliance on bad utilitarian arguments to justify their actions. The redefined approach to international marketing would have encouraged the company to attempt, at the onset of the marketing effort, to determine the overall effect that the marketing of one of its products would have on the economy of the developing country and on those who live within the country.

The viability of this approach rests on the fact that it is preventative rather than corrective in nature. Indeed, questions of profits, market share and target marketing should come only after the TNC has determined whether it is morally responsible for them to produce and market a given product in a developing country. In developing countries, questions of a moral nature are bound to be raised when TNCs decide to market products mainly because there exists a demand. While the TNC profits from such situations, the economy, and ultimately the individuals within the society, run all the risk. Any damage to the economy of the developing country is sure to injure the well-being of those who live in those countries. In such situations, it could be argued that, under the social contract, the

FIGURE 3. Ethical Decision Making Framework.

<u>Situation</u>	<u>Ethical Approach</u>	<u>Decision Rules</u>	<u>+ ives/ – ives</u>
	SOCIAL CONTRACT – (What's ethical depends upon the social contract between the TNC and the host country)	Can action be consistently undertaken as a general rule? – Does action minimize drawbacks associated with productive organizations? – Does action refrain from violating minimum standards of justice and human rights, i.e., duties to respect human rights of workers and consumers in host country? – Does action remain faithful to the contract? – Does action benefit host country? (Note: Good cannot be traded off against harm) – Does action respect human rights of workers and consumers in the host country? – Does action fulfill duties of beneficence, i.e., does it improve lives in LDCs? – Does action avoid intentional direct harm? – Does action promote development of just background institutions within the host country and internationally? – Does action respect the laws of of the host country? – Does action respect the culture of the host country? – Where human rights are not violated, does action respect the values of the host country? – Do well-defined norms take priority over more general, less precise norms? – Does action meet spirit and letter of the law in situations where there is conflict among norms? – Are interactions between the firm and individuals compatible with societal norms? **[IF ANSWERS = YES the act is ethical]**	+ Enhance long term welfare of stakeholders + Obligation not to do harm

TNC may be irresponsible in the performance of its positive as well as its negative duties.

By contrast, the actions of the Caterpillar Tractor Company can be used to illustrate the viability of the macro approach to international marketing in developing countries. In this case the company sets priorities that will guide actions in the field. While the Tractor Company is undoubtedly concerned with its market share and profitability, it has also taken steps to ensure that the human and natural resources of the developing country are developed. At the same time, the safety standards enacted are similar to those used in developed countries. From a moral standpoint, the company makes no attempt to profit at the expense of an unsuspecting or disempowered developing country (Bowie, 1982).

Generally, corporations argue that they are in business for the purpose of making profits and the obligation to ensure some minimum standard of living falls to the host government of the developing country. While this statement is partly accurate in that the social contract requires that the corporation receive benefits, the TNC violates the social contract when its behavior is inconsistent with the "moral minimum" of not causing avoidable harm. Bowie (1982) argues that the corporations' contract with society allows the corporation to maximize profits so long as profit-making does not cause avoidable harm.

From a corporate policy perspective, it is imperative for TNCs to adhere to universal moral norms of justice or fair play (Rawls, 1971). As a party to the social contract, the TNC should regard a developing country as an end in and of itself and not merely as a means to an end. Thus, while the developing country recognizes the right of the TNC to make a profit, the TNC must also recognize that it has a responsibility not to act in ways that prevent the host country from growing in real terms. It should be noted, however, that this scenario can work very nicely only if there are no conflicts of interest among the countries within which the TNC is operating. If there are such conflicts of interest, then a potentially unsolvable conundrum may arise in the relationship.

An argument against moral obligations arising from a social contract might be based on the assertion that corporations do not have rights as do individuals. However, the civil laws which make

TNCs possible are those which grant rights and obligations to individuals (Ewing, 1984). For TNCs, the right to operate in the developing country is partially grounded in the civil arrangements made possible by the social contract that exists between the individual and the state. If the corporation wishes to have rights, it becomes necessary, by extension, to adhere to the obligations which accompany those rights.

THE MORAL OBLIGATIONS
OF TRANSNATIONAL CORPORATIONS

In developing countries, the moral obligation of the TNC is owed to the state or economy as an entity and also to the individuals within that economy. From this perspective, Furuhashi and McCarthy (1981) note that transnational marketing may be conceived of as involving both the TNC's interaction with its various individual and institutional customers (micro level), and the interaction with the developing country as the consumer (macro level). Because TNCs are often able to control the market resources (labor and capital) of developing countries, there is a need to focus on their activities in an attempt to assess how their actions are related to issues concerned with market effectiveness, ethics, and morality.

McCarthy (1981) notes that no economic system is likely to achieve its macro level objectives without an effective micro marketing system. It is for this very reason that the interaction between the developing countries and the TNC takes on obligations that far exceed the realm of marketing and economics. TNCs operating in less developed countries are often able to control more than just the product, price, place and promotion (4P's). The political, legal, economic, technological, competitive, and in some cases even the social environment, may be controlled by the TNC. Where the uncontrollable variables become controllables to the TNC, the developing country is at a great disadvantage. In such situations the TNC needs to be guided, not only by economic and market constructs, but also by constructs arising out of the social contract with the developing country.

In exchange for providing land, labor and markets for TNCs, developing countries generally hope to receive a transfer of technology, marketing ideas, product research and development, product export and export substitution, employment, and an adherence to social and ethical constructs that do not stifle growth of the developing country and its citizens. Therefore, TNCs must look to the emergence of marketing patterns which fulfill the moral conditions of their social contracts with the developing countries. Such outcomes would feed back into the home country of the TNC as well as into the host society of the developing country. This would bring about change and improvement at the level of the social institutions and lead to a more enlightened sphere of transnational marketing.

That the consumer in the developing economy lacks "western-style" sovereignty places a greater obligation upon the TNC. Additionally, TNCs have role-specific obligations that go well beyond profits and the obligations perceived by law. These role-specific obligations exist because of the perceived importance of the TNC to the economic vitality of the developing country. This could be measured in terms of the effect that TNCs have on all aspects of life in the developing country.

The responsibilities of TNCs could therefore be viewed as being of a normative but hierarchical nature rather than being relative or utilitarian. The nature and size of the markets in developing countries, coupled with the size and power of TNCs, inherently place greater than normal obligations on TNCs. Given no final regulatory body, TNCs, by necessity, are expected to live up to their moral obligation to the developing countries. That is, TNCs operating in developing countries are expected to develop internal decision-making procedures which take their obligations under these into account and to do more than just meet their negative duties (Donaldson and Dunfee, 1994; Donaldson, 1985; Goodpaster, 1984; Goodpaster and Matthews, 1982; Garrett, 1966).

Some examples will help illustrate the nature of the social contract between TNCs and developing countries. In the much discussed "Marketing Infant Formula" (Velasquez, 1982), the Nestle company carried out marketing practices which, though not illegal, by most accounts left much to be desired. Because of Nestle's actions in developing countries, numerous incidences of diarrhea, malnutrition, and death occurred among babies. It was estimated that infant deaths attributable to the infant formula might have been as high as ten million per year. The moral question is whether Nestle could have done anything to prevent or reduce these health hazards. It could be debatable whether the prevention of health hazards is of a higher moral priority than the profit performance of a TNC. It took more than seven years for the Nestle conflict to be settled. However, during this period, the company continued to market its products to developing countries. In this respect, the Nestle company responded to neither its positive moral obligations to do good and prevent harm nor its negative moral obligations to avoid causing harm. It seems reasonable for developing societies to expect TNCs not to cause harm and to make efforts to prevent harm, given that it is within their control to do so.

The many problems of TNCs operating in both the pharmaceutical and the chemical industries also highlight ethical issues and the wider problem of getting TNCs to act in a manner that enhances the public good in developing countries. For example, TNCs export hazardous chemicals and drugs to developing countries without full warning. Arguing that any risks are far outweighed by the benefits, an industry spokesperson noted that the chemicals are needed in developing countries to grow food, and the drugs are needed for healthier lives (Rose, 1992; Smith and Quelch, 1991b; Scanlan, 1991b, 1991c).

By contrast, the Caterpillar Tractor Company actually adopted an international code that guided company actions in situations where conflict of interest existed. By enacting a self-regulating code, the company gave preference to such issues as using "local" sources of supply, uniformity in product design and quality, and responsibility in employment, promotion and pricing (Bowie, 1982). Consequently, Caterpillar is perceived to utilize codes of international business ethics to promote a responsible basis for operations in developing countries.

CONCLUSION

The conceptual framework that we have put forward in this paper attempts to address the ethical concerns that are likely to arise because of the relationship between TNCs and developing countries. By allowing for a combination of both the macro and micro factors that affect the relationship, the social contract perspective offers a more comprehensive approach to studying the ethical implications of the TNC-developing country interaction. The approach represents an opportunity for managers to make ethically sound decisions. The framework can assist management in deciding what ethical criteria to employ. As such, this study offers a pragmatic theoretical framework setting forth a process for making sound judgements in business ethics. By helping to establish contractual norms, the approach also enables managers to assess the degree to which individuals within the firm act in accordance with the social contract.

Even as it seeks to limit the range of norms under consideration, this article provides a schema that establishes a means for displaying and assessing the ethical relevance of existing norms in societies, markets, corporations, and other economic communities. As such, the social contract perspective seeks to go beyond the generality of deontology and utilitarianism to provide for a more detailed normative assessment of the particular ethical problems of transnational economic life. By addressing issues of relevance with respect to existing cultural and economic norms, this study also provides an agenda for future theoretical and empirical research that should entail the search for authentic ethical norms in business ranging from interactions within or between industries, corporations, alliances, and regional and international socioeconomic systems.

As a possible guide to the actions of TNCs, the social contract framework enables us to evaluate the performance of TNCs against a set of established norms that are so fundamental to human existence that they serve as a guide in evaluating lower level moral norms (Donaldson and Dunfee, 1994). Although the thrust of the paper has been placed upon the business activities of TNCs in developing countries, the concepts presented are universal in nature and are applicable to business activities across the globe.

Three major points have been argued in this paper: (1) the need exists for a comprehensive approach to thinking about and implementing the tenets of the marketing concept in transnational marketing to developing countries; (2) the social contract framework presents a viable means of evaluating the actions of transnational corporations operating in developing countries; and (3) beyond the mere satisfaction of individual needs, it is necessary for TNCs to operate in a manner such that the needs of the developing country, as the ultimate consumer, would be satisfied.

In their operation in developing countries, it is important, as a moral imperative, for TNCs to look beyond the need for profits alone. It is possible for TNCs to structure their activities to satisfy the needs and wants of developing economies such that significant profits and growth are conceivable in the long-run. To view their business activities in developing countries primarily as sources of profits provides a less than morally defensible position and sends the wrong signal to developing countries. Indeed, some developing countries might perceive TNCs as corporations that view the citizens of developing countries as merely the means by which TNCs, and industrialized countries, can improve their profits and their balance of payments, while widening the economic gap between developed and developing countries.

Any claim that the TNC has a right to exist must rest on a theory of the marketplace which recognizes that TNCs, while enriching themselves, also have an obligation to enhance, if not to enrich, the countries in which they operate. By enhancing the economic and social prosperity of the countries in which they do business, TNCs are well positioned to elevate their market position. Failure to adopt this perspective will, in the long-run, cause TNCs to forfeit their right to enter and operate in developing countries.

The ethical perspective provided in this paper deserves further critical analysis. Future empirical research efforts are needed to enhance our understanding of ethics and transnational corporate moral responsibility as it affects developing countries. Only through such efforts can we achieve a greater appreciation of this important dimension of business activity across national boundaries.

AUTHOR NOTES

Hudson P. Rogers teaches courses in Consumer Behavior, Marketing Management, and International Marketing and International Business. Apart from having his work published in such journals as the *Journal of Teaching for International Business, Journal of International Business Studies, Journal of Marketing for Higher Education, Journal of Consumer Satisfaction/Dissatisfaction and Complaining Behavior, Journal of Education for Business, Journal of Personal Selling and Sales Management*, and the *Journal of Marketing Education*, he has published and presented articles at numerous conferences.

Alphonso O. Ogbuehi teaches courses in Marketing Management, and International Marketing. Dr. Ogbuehi has published in such journals as the *Journal of Global Marketing, Journal of Marketing Channels, Journal of Applied Business Research, Journal of Marketing for Higher Education, Journal of Education for Business, International Marketing Review*, and the *Journal of Marketing Education*. He has also published numerous articles on conference proceedings.

C. M. Kochunny teaches courses in Advertising, International Marketing, and Consumer Behavior. He has published in such journals as the *Journal of Marketing Education, Journal of Education for Business, Journal of Teaching for International Business*, and the *Journal of International Consumer Marketing*. Dr. Kochunny has also published numerous articles on conference proceedings.

REFERENCES

Armstrong, R. W., Stening, B. W., Ryans, J. K., and Mayo, M. (1990). International Marketing Ethics: Problems Encountered by Australian Firms, *European Journal of Marketing*, (October), 5-19.

Barnet, Richard J. and Muller, Ronald E. (1974). *Global Reach: The Power of the Multinational Corporations*. New York, New York: Simon and Schuster.

Beauchamp, Tom L. and Bowie, Norman E. (1988). *Ethical Theory and Business*. Englewood Cliffs: Prentice-Hall, Inc.

Boatright, John R. (1993). *Ethics and the Conduct of Business*. Englewood Cliffs, New Jersey: Prentice-Hall, Inc.

Bogan, Michael (1979). International Trade and the New Swedish Provisions on Corruption, *American Journal of Comparative Law*, 29 (Fall), 660-667.

Bowie, Norman (1990). Business Ethics and Cultural Relativism. In Nadsen, Peter and Shafritz, Jay M. (Eds). *Essentials of Business Ethics*, 366-382.

Bowie, Norman E. (1982). *Business Ethics*. Englewood Cliffs, New Jersey: Prentice-Hall, Inc.

Bull, David (1982). *A Growing Problem*. Oxford, England: OXFAM.

Buller, Paul F., Kohls, John J., and Anderson, Kenneth S. (1991). The Challenge of Global Ethics, *Journal of Business Ethics*, 10 (October), 767-775.

Cavanagh, Gerald F. (1984). *American Business Values*. Englewood Cliffs, New Jersey: Prentice-Hall, Inc.

Cavusgil, S. Tamer and Nevin, John R. (1981). State-of-the-Art in International Marketings: An Assessment. In Enis, Ben M. and Roering, Kenneth J. (Eds.), *Review of Marketing 1981*. American Marketing Association, 195-216.

Cross, Frank B. and Winslett, Brenda J. (1987). "Export Death": Ethical Issues and the International Trade in Hazardous Products, *American Business Law Journal*, (Fall), 487-521.

De George, Richard T. (1990). *Business Ethics*. New York: MacMillan Publishing Company.

De George, Richard T. (1986). Ethical Dilemmas for Multinational Enterprise: A

Philosophical Overview. In Hoffman, W. Michael, Lange, Ann E. and Fedo, David A. (Eds.), *Ethics and the Multinational Enterprise,* 39-46.

Donaldson, Thomas (1989). Social Contracts and Corporations: A Reply to Hodapp, *Journal of Business Ethics,* (8), 133-137.

Donaldson, Thomas (1985). Multinational Decision-Making: Reconciling International Norms, *Journal of Business Ethics,* (4), 357-366.

Donaldson, Thomas, (1982). Constructing a Social Contract for Business. In Donaldson, Thomas (Ed.), *Corporations and Morality.*

Donaldson, Thomas and Thomas W. Dunfee (1994). Toward a Unified Conception of Business Ethics: Integrative Social Contract Theory, *The Academy of Management Review,* (April), 252-284.

Donaldson, Thomas and Patricia H. Werhane (1988). *Ethical Issues in Business: A Philosophical Approach,* Englewood Cliffs, NJ: Prentice-Hall.

Dunfee, Thomas W. (1991). Business Ethics and Extant Social Contracts. *Business Ethics Quarterly,* (1), 23-51.

Ewing, D. W. (1984). *Freedom Inside the Organization.* New York: McGraw-Hill.

Fasching, Darrell J. (1981). A Case for Corporate and Management Ethics, *California Management Review,* 23 (Summer), 62-76.

Fortune (1988). The World's 50 Biggest International Business Corporations, August 1, D3.

Friedman, Milton (1970). The Social Responsibility of Business is to Increase its Profits, *New York Times Magazine,* (September, 13), 32-33, 122-126.

Friedman, Milton (1962). *Capitalism and Freedom.* Chicago: University of Chicago Press.

Furuhashi, Y. H. and McCarthy, E. J. (1981). *Social Issues of Marketing in the American Economy.* Columbus, Ohio: Grid, Inc.

Garrett, Thomas M. (1966). *Business Ethics.* New York, New York: Appleton-Century-Crofts.

Goodpaster, Kenneth E. (1984). The Concept of Corporate Responsibility. In Regan, Tom (Ed.), *New Introductory Essays in Business Ethics.*

Goodpaster, Kenneth E., and John B. Matthews, Jr. (1982). Can a Corporation Have a Conscience? *Harvard Business Review,* (January/February).

Gough, John W. (1957). *The Social Contract,* 2nd ed., Oxford: The Clarendon Press.

Hoffman, Michael W., Lange, Ann E., and Fedo, David A., Eds. (1986). *Ethics and the Multinational Enterprise,* Washington, DC: University Press of America.

Kaikati, Jack and Wayne A. Label (1980). American Bribery Legislation: An Obstacle to International Marketing, *Journal of Marketing,* 44 (Fall), 38-43.

Keeley, M. (1988). *A Social Contract Theory of Organizations.* Notre Dame, IN: University of Notre Dame Press.

Laczniak, Gene R. and Naor, Jacob (1985). Global Ethics: Wrestling with the Corporate Conscience, *Business* (35), 3-8.

Lazer, William (1969). Marketing's Changing Social Relationships, *Journal of Marketing,* 33 (January), 3-9.

Levitt, Theodore (1983). The Globalization of Markets, *Harvard Business Review*, (May-June).

Mason, Kenneth W. (1979). Responsibility for What's on the Tube, *Business Week*, (August 13), 14.

McCarthy, E. J. (1981). *Basic Marketing*. Homewood, Illinois: Richard D. Irwin, Inc.

Mills, John S. (1957). *Utilitarianism*. Indianapolis: Bobbs-Merrill.

Morris, M. (1985). Moral Constraints, Prisoners' Dilemmas, and the Social Responsibilities of Corporations. In *Profit and Responsibility*, Patricia H. Werhane and K. D'Andrade, eds., Englewood Cliffs, NJ: Prentice-Hall, pp. 116-119.

Rawls, John (1971). *A Theory of Justice*. Cambridge, Massachusetts: Belknap Press.

Robin, Donald P. (1992). Research and Analysis in Marketing Ethics: Directions and Opportunities, *Journal of Marketing Theory and Practice*, (Fall), 22-30.

Rose, Robert L. (1992). Breast Implants Still Being Sold Outside U. S., *The Wall Street Journal*, (Wednesday, March 4), B1, B5.

Scanlan, Christopher (1991a). Medicines Banned at Home Sold by U. S. Makers Abroad, *The Miami Herald*. (May 29), 11A.

Scanlan, Christopher (1991b). U. S. Barred Products Sold Abroad, *The Miami Herald*. (May 27), 13A.

Scanlan, Christopher (1991c). U. S. Pesticide Brings Death to a Tiny Village, *The Miami Herald*, (May 28), 16-17A.

Sethi, S. Prakash (1975). Dimensions of Corporate Social Performance: An Analytical Framework, *California Management Review*, (Spring), 58-64.

Silverman, Milton, Philip R. Lee, and Mia Lydecker (1986). Drug Promotion: The Third World Revisited, *International Journal of Health Services*, 16 (4).

Silverman, Milton, Philip R. Lee, and Mia Lydecker (1982). The Drugging of the Third World, *International Journal of Health Services*, 12 (4).

Smith, N. Craig and John A. Quelch (1991a). *Ethics in Marketing*. Homewood, IL: Irwin.

Smith, N. Craig and John A. Quelch (1991b). Pharmaceutical Marketing Practices in the Third World, *Journal of Business Research*, 23 (August), 113-126.

Velasquez, Manuel G. (1982). *Business Ethics: Concepts and Cases*. Englewood Cliffs, New Jersey: Prentice-Hall, Inc.

Wall Street Journal (1989). Thailand, Malaysia Set for Economic Takeoff, Vol. 120, No. 122C, A8.

White, Thomas I. (1993). *Business Ethics: A Philosophical Reader*. New York: MacMillan Publishing Company.

The Impact
of International Gray Marketing
on Consumers and Firms

Lynette Knowles Mathur

SUMMARY. This article examines the relationship of marketing ethics, as a subset of business ethics, to international gray markets for consumer goods and, thus, addresses a gap in the gray marketing and international marketing literatures. The paper first briefly covers gray markets and provides examples of gray market consumer goods. It then presents a framework through a discussion of marketing ethics and identification of marketing ethics issues relative to gray marketing. The third section addresses the relationship of the external authorized channel and causes of gray marketing with reference to marketing ethics and cross-cultural effects. Finally, implications for consumers, authorized firms, and society in general are given.

INTRODUCTION

Marketing goods to consumers through external marketing channels has existed for hundreds of years. So, too, have criticisms in certain segments of society regarding business ethics, especially

Lynette Knowles Mathur, PhD, is Assistant Professor of Marketing in the College of Business and Administration, Southern Illinois University at Carbondale, Carbondale, IL 62901.

She thanks two anonymous reviewers and Professor Nejdet Delener for their insightful comments on earlier drafts of the paper.

[Haworth co-indexing entry note]: "The Impact of International Gray Marketing on Consumers and Firms." Mathur, Lynette Knowles. Co-published simultaneously in the *Journal of Euromarketing* (International Business Press, an imprint of The Haworth Press, Inc.) Vol. 4, No. 2, 1995, pp. 39-59; and: *Ethical Issues in International Marketing* (ed: Nejdet Delener) International Business Press, an imprint of The Haworth Press, Inc., 1995, pp. 39-59. Multiple copies of this article/chapter may be purchased from The Haworth Document Delivery Center [1-800-3-HAWORTH; 9:00 a.m. - 5:00 p.m. (EST)].

39

those that directly affect consumer well-being (Becker and Fritzsche, 1987). Business ethics has received greater attention in recent years. Analyzing ethics involves a system of principles and a definition of right and wrong, which are applied to actual or potential ethical problems (Cooke, 1991; Getz, 1990; Raibom and Payne, 1990), such as those associated with business issues. Analyzing business ethics recognizes the legality and the full degree of perceived ethicality of business issues because an issue's legality, generally based on society's belief in right or wrong, does not always reflect the full degree of its perceived ethicality (Cooke, 1991; Raibom and Payne, 1990). Further, business ethics of individuals and firms should be examined jointly since they shape and affect one another through a series of iterations (Epstein, 1989). Lastly, analyzing business ethics should address stakeholders to whom business has fiduciary responsibilities, i.e., managers, shareholders, employees, suppliers, customers, consumers, and, finally, society, because it is the largest group and because it is society that allows business to exist (Gandz and Hayes, 1988; Laczniak and Murphy, 1993; Raibom and Payne, 1990).

This paper examines the relationship of marketing ethics to international gray markets for consumer goods. A gray market is an external marketing channel that is unauthorized by the manufacturer. It is "gray" because, although it is generally legal, its ethicality is uncertain.[1] In gray marketing, a "diverter," a firm in the authorized marketing channel (the channel), sells authorized goods to a "gray marketer," an unauthorized reseller, making them "gray market goods."[2] Diverting violates a traditional business assumption that firms, and business people, will behave ethically, honor contracts, and deal fairly (Gandz and Hayes, 1988). Gray marketing has potential consumer risks that may be costly and may lessen control in the channel over marketing strategy, reducing performance and benefits to society.

The gray marketing literature addresses virtually only international gray markets. Most gray markets are international and most gray market goods are from international channels, although, on occasion, domestic goods may be diverted. Gray marketing is part of international marketing in terms of the channel and importing/exporting. Henceforth, "gray market," "gray marketing," and "channel" refer to international forms in this paper.

Because of the international dimensions, this paper addresses cross-cultural aspects of marketing ethics and gray marketing. Certain cross-cultural issues have been examined in the literature on marketing ethics. However, as Wines and Napier (1992) have pointed out, research on cross-cultural ethics is constrained by problems in separately examining culture, morality, and ethics, and in agreeing about universal moral values. Research has focused on ethical codes of conduct, managers' attitudes, and national character (Becker and Fritzsche, 1987; Laczniak and Murphy, 1991; Langlois and Schlegelmilch, 1990; Raibom and Payne, 1990; Tsalikis and Fritzsche, 1989), ethics judgments and country differences (Whipple and Swords, 1992), ethics in marketing research (Akaah, 1990), business students' ethics (Lysonski, 1991), ethics in organizational development (White and Rhodeback, 1992), and model building (Wines and Napier, 1992). However, the literature has not covered the relationship of marketing ethics to gray marketing. Thus, the purpose of this paper is to examine this issue.

The gray marketing literature has directly addressed its legality, including protecting consumers and trademark owners (Minehan, 1991). Legal implications for U.S. firms have been addressed for over 100 years (Cross et al., 1992). Gray marketing is illegal when imported gray market goods violate either product regulations or a licensing contract for the trademark's use in a foreign country (Cianci, 1988). However, this situation applies only to 10 percent of gray market sales (Dwyer, 1988). Most firms in the U.S. are not legally protected from gray marketing and must rely more strongly on reference to ethical issues. However, the attention to marketing ethics that is found in the gray marketing literature has been meager and is limited to general business media (e.g., Lozano, 1988), with virtually no treatment in academic journals. This paper addresses that void in the literature.

This paper is organized as follows. The first part presents gray markets and examples of gray market consumer goods. The second section discusses marketing ethics, identifies marketing ethics issues related to gray marketing, and presents a framework of ethical decision-making relative to gray marketing. The third part addresses the relationship of the external authorized channel and causes of gray marketing with reference to marketing ethics and cross-cultural effects. The fourth section discusses the implications. The final part presents the conclusions.

INTERNATIONAL GRAY MARKETS

Gray markets in total have an estimated annual value from $7 billion to $10 billion (Cavusgil and Sikora, 1988; Cespedes et al., 1988). Gray market goods enter through countries other than the country of origin or final market, or through direct export from the country of origin, also known as "parallel importing." Gray market consumer goods (see Table 1) span mostly well-known brand names and vary in technology, e.g., cameras versus liquors, and serialization, e.g., automobiles versus perfumes.

Causes for gray markets are discussed in detail in a later section. In general, gray market goods are characterized by high resale potential, trade-marked brand names, good market recognition, and established price and performance. They can be readily stored, inventoried, and distributed. They are easily transferred across political boundaries and may have multilingual packaging.

TABLE 1. Examples of Gray Market Goods*

- -

automobiles (e.g., Mercedes-Benz), tires
cameras (e.g., Olympus), camera film (e.g., Fuji), photographic equipment
personal computers (e.g., IBM), software (e.g., Lotus)
batteries (e.g., Duracell)
audiotapes, electronic equipment (e.g., Hewlett-Packard), telephones (e.g., Panasonic)
contact lenses, cosmetics, hair care products, drugs,** toothpaste
liquor (e.g., Bailey's Irish Cream, Cutty-Sark Scotch, Suntory Old-Japan)
perfume and cologne (e.g., Chanel, Charles of the Ritz, Opium, Old Spice)
watches (e.g., Cartier, Rolex, Swatch Watch)
apparel
glassware, fine china
soft drinks (e.g., Coke, Sprite), food (e.g., Spam)

- -

*   Sources: Armstrong, 1988; Cavusgil and Sikora, 1988; Cespedes et al., 1988; Cianci, 1988; Commins, 1990; Duhan and Sheffet, 1988; Dwyer and Dunkin, 1988; Engardio et al., 1988; Gannon, 1991; Honigsbaum, 1988; Howell et al., 1986; Lozano, 1988; Ludwig and Koenig, 1990; Maskulka and Gulas, 1987; Meyerowitz, 1986; Serko, 1986; Weigand, 1991.
** Because of actual and potential problems of gray market drugs, Congress passed legislation making it illegal, in most cases, to import drugs purchased in foreign countries, even U.S.-made ones (Engardio et al., 1988).

MARKETING ETHICS

Marketing activities tend to be at the core of business decision making. They are also the part of the firm's operations that are most exposed to the firm's external environment and, as such, are under the greatest pressure to deviate from accepted norms of behavior (Ferrell and Gresham, 1985). Because of this exposure and pressure to deviate, many business ethics issues involve marketing decision-making. Further, by its very nature, the channel as a system is open to environmental influences (Rosenbloom, 1991) and, thus, is susceptible to pressure to deviate in behavior, such as with gray marketing.

There are several sources of conflict in marketing ethics that affect the external authorized channel and take on added significance in international marketing. These sources of ethical conflict may provide the environment and opportunities for gray marketing.

The most frequent source of conflict in marketing ethics for marketing managers is the lack of congruence between corporate and customer interests (Chonko and Hunt, 1985). Ethical problems in the channel may result from salesforce conflict with short- and long-term objectives, which represent corporate interests (Tsalikis and Fritzsche, 1989). Salesforce conflict with the objectives may arise through problems with sales management ethics, which often involve the setting of sales quotas that sales people may perceive as unfair and threatening their financial remuneration (Laczniak and Murphy, 1993). Corporate interests often focus on economic factors, such as objectives to increase sales, reduce costs, and increase profits, because managers often think in terms of economic criteria (Laczniak and Murphy, 1991). It is recognized that economic factors may affect ethical decision-making in marketing (Akaah, 1992). However, their effect may vary greatly in the international arena due to their diversity and influence on business behavior. For example, aspects of capitalist and socialist economic systems affect the cultural values toward work and wealth and, thus, the attitudes and perspectives of business people differently.

Although ethical issues in international marketing may be quite complex to start with, they may assume added significance if business people do not have sufficiently broad cross-cultural perspectives. This lack of breadth in perspective may create ethical conflict.

For example, enculturation may affect the behavior of managers and sales people in international channels. Values toward time, work, wealth, achievement, and change are formed by enculturation (Terpstra and David, 1991) and affect decision-making, behavior, and performance. However, enculturation causes a natural degree of bias toward that culture, which, if left to its own means, may lead to ethnocentrism (Czinkota et al., 1994; Harris and Moran, 1987). Ethnocentrism, in turn, may cause managers and sales people to work under the assumption that marketing ethics are the same across all cultures.

Several aspects of the relationship of marketing ethics to international gray marketing are examined within the following discussion of the external authorized channel and causes of international gray marketing: how marketing strategy in the channel deviates to contribute to gray marketing; economic pressures in the channel that affect management decision-making regarding marketing ethics and gray marketing; parts of marketing strategy in the channel that relate to marketing ethics and gray marketing; and behaviors of managers and sales people in the channel that contribute to problems with marketing ethics and gray marketing.

CAUSES OF GRAY MARKETING

This section examines the causes of gray marketing as related to channel activities by addressing diverters and gray marketers, and the marketing strategy.

Diverters and Gray Marketers

Diverters are usually intermediaries, although manufacturers infrequently divert (Honigsbaum, 1988). Diverting is usually intentional, but unintentional diverting may occur when an authorized salesforce acts independently from management and diverts (Honigsbaum, 1988), an authorized firm is defrauded by a gray marketer[3] (Engardio et al., 1988), or an authorized firm unethically pressures an authorized buyer to over-order and the buyer then diverts excess inventory (Meyerowitz, 1986). Intentional diverters and gray marketers usually engage in gray marketing because of their own economic pressures (Cespedes et al., 1988; Engardio et al., 1988).

Marketing Strategy

Marketing strategy in the channel may contribute to gray marketing in terms of authorized goods, target markets, pricing, ordering, salesforce, and channel control. A successful strategy often attracts and unintentionally supports gray marketers who "free-ride" on the strategy by relying on it for market coverage, without permission or economic investment. Although "free-riding" is not illegal, it is basically unethical since gray marketers are "squatters" on the channel, using authorized goods, the strategy, and firms' identities to achieve their own objectives.

Authorized goods and brand names are valuable assets that the manufacturer often protects with patents, trademarks,[4] and controls over pricing, quality, and peripheral aspects–such as warranties–"bundled" with the good. The assets may be used in brand name extensions over new products to ensure intermediaries that they will generate acceptable profits. Prices, usually based on quality and market recognition, may also be set relative to market prices, intermediaries' profit margins, order quantities, price/quantity schedules, and peripheral aspects. Further, prices are often differentiated across markets and countries due to price/quantity schedules and to differences in consumer demand, culture, pricing, foreign exchange, distribution, transportation, and so on.

Authorized goods as future gray market goods have higher resale potential, in terms of characteristics, performance, and product life cycle (PLC), that provides flexibility in gray market sourcing or sales (Cespedes et al., 1988; Duhan and Sheffet, 1988; Howell et al., 1986). They have trade-marked brand names and established price, performance, and market recognition that ensure demand and minimize consumer education. They have good market transferability since they can be stored and inventoried, may have multilingual packaging, and are often standardized across markets and sold in countries with low trade barriers. Their differentiated prices, the most common cause of gray marketing (Engardio et al., 1988), allow gray marketers to source where authorized prices are lower and sell where gray market prices are higher, but competitive[5] (Engardio et al., 1988). Differentiated pricing due to price/quantity schedules allow resellers to buy excess goods at a lower cost and divert extra inventory.

Future gray market goods may depend on the maturity stage of their PLCs (Cespedes et al., 1988). In this stage, consumer familiarity with the product category may increase price sensitivity, diminish their value of product support and peripheral aspects "bundled" with the good, and cause them to seek lower prices and "unbundled" goods not found in the channel. PLC variability among countries may increase gray marketing since goods in the maturity stage in one country may be sold in other countries where the PLC is younger and the goods are unavailable.

Limits of the manufacturer's target market, due to market selection, expansion, and distribution, may cause product unavailability, inaccessibility to authorized resellers, and unwillingness or inability to pay set prices. Consumers may search for unauthorized firms with goods at competitive prices. Gray marketers may view a lack of market focus by the channel as an advantageous supply and demand imbalance (Cavusgil and Sikora, 1988). Major changes in consumer buying behavior may also create gray marketing opportunities, such as increased demand for lower-priced goods, which may be encouraged by governments (Armstrong, 1988).

Advertising for brand-named consumer goods is usually used to "pull" the goods through the channel and usually identifies and relates images and values of goods, brand names, and authorized firms. Advertising is a common part of the marketing strategy that gray marketers "free-ride" to educate consumers about goods and minimize their advertising costs.

Ordering policies are used in the channel with pricing policies, e.g., order quantities and price/quantity schedules, to ensure optimum and manageable inventory levels. Sellers may not allow order changes or cancellations because of potential negative effects on inventory management and production. This lack of flexibility may cause intermediaries to divert when faced with unforeseen changes, such as declines in consumer demand.

Sales people are usually used to "push" the good through the channel. Salesforce performance expectations may contribute to gray marketing. Performance expectations are often based on the quantity sold, which may be measured against a sales quota and may be affected by order quantities, price/quantity schedules, and the "bundling" of peripheral aspects. Sales people may have to deal with conflicting short- and long-term corporate objectives, e.g., short-term sales quotas versus long-term customer confidence and satisfaction. They may view sales quotas as unfair (Laczniak and Murphy, 1993) and, thus, divert to meet objectives and achieve acceptable performances. Further, because of cultural-specific values and group expectations and norms, sales people across cultures may have different perceptions about the fairness of objectives and acceptable performances and, thus, view diverting differently.

Diverters may violate explicit and implicit contracts in the channel that are used for channel control. Channel control is the management of channel activities to ensure efficiency and effectiveness (Rosenbloom, 1991). It is more difficult, especially in international marketing, with increased channel complexity, which is levels, types, and numbers of intermediaries, and environmental complexity, which is often due to differences in cultural aspects, consumer demand, pricing, foreign exchange, competition, distribution, and transportation.

Agreements are used by firms for channel control to indicate legitimate rights in relationships with other firms (Rosenbloom, 1991) and to express a degree of marketing ethics in the expectations. Legitimacy, which differs across cultures as a form of power, focuses on positions in firms, e.g., managers or salespeople, and requires that those positions give their continuing consent (Terpstra and David, 1991). It exists when a firm's internalized norms dictate that another firm has a right to influence it and it must accept that influence (Rosenbloom, 1991).

Explicit and implicit contracts are agreements commonly used in channels to indicate marketing strategy parameters, e.g., using only high-end retailers. Explicit contracts are legally enforceable, at a cost (Dobson, 1990), but the cost may be greater in international marketing due to differences in legal systems, such as code law versus common law, and in cultural influences on national laws and their use, such as litigation in the U.S. versus settling conflict outside courts in Japan (Czinkota et al., 1994). To avoid high legal costs, firms usually use implicit contracts (Dobson, 1990), but they have enforcement problems since they are generally unwritten, may be vague, and are not easily enforced at a reasonable cost (Dobson, 1990). These problems usually increase in international marketing because of cultural differences, such as languages and high-context versus low-context cultures (Czinkota et al., 1994; Hall, 1989), and the relevant meanings and importance of agreements. Instead, implicit contracts must be enforced through ethics (Dobson, 1990); however, complexities of cross-cultural ethics make this difficult.

The risk of diverting may be partly caused by the manufacturer if it did not understand cross-cultural aspects of its intermediaries to clearly know when, how, and to what degree they regard agreements as legitimate and binding. This problem, perhaps due to management's ethnocentric attitudes, may lead the manufacturer to mistakenly conclude that intermediaries that divert have deficiencies in marketing ethics when, in fact, the problem may be due to lack of understanding of cross-cultural ethics.

IMPLICATIONS OF INTERNATIONAL GRAY MARKETING

Implications of international gray marketing for consumers and firms, relative to marketing ethics, are examined in the two main areas of marketing strategy and management orientation.

Marketing Strategy

Gray marketing may reduce the long-term effectiveness of marketing strategy in the channel, causing marketing results to be less meaningfully related to marketing resources, thereby reducing operating cost efficiency. Resources such as marketing research and capital may be affected, especially when more research may be needed to learn about gray marketing.

The use of resources, such as marketing research and capital, to fight gray marketing reduces the availability of inputs to produce marketing outputs, such as improved product development and selection. Hence, it diminishes the possible societal benefits from marketing outputs, such as improved standard of living and utilization of income. It can be argued that marketing strategy should be responsible to society since, as indicated earlier, business is allowed by society to exist, has fiduciary responsibility to society, and both causes and is affected by societal changes. However, when society allows gray marketing to exist, both business and society may be negatively affected and the problem may become more complex due to cross-cultural aspects of social responsibility, e.g., the valuation of societal benefits in different cultures.

Gray marketing may damage the images and values of goods and brand names, thus reducing their usefulness in the channel and to consumers and society. It may lessen the effectiveness of pricing strategy in the channel because gray market goods are lower-price alternatives and may cause consumers to be suspicious about the pricing of authorized firms (Cavusgil and Sikora, 1988). It may also cause goods to be distributed excessively or without services otherwise provided by authorized firms, thus hurting product images (Cavusgil and Sikora, 1988; Lowe and McCrohan, 1989). For example, excessive distribution and reduced prices of gray market Cartier watches and Chanel perfumes seriously diminished their images (Serko, 1986; Weigand, 1991). Consumers may also believe that authorized firms sell unsafe, damaged, or obsolete goods, or consumers may be unaware of product recalls (Duhan and Sheffet, 1988; Lowe and McCrohan, 1989). For example, gray market Duracell batteries may be shipped excessive distances in gray marketing channels, coming to consumers old and diminished in quality (Lowe and McCrohan, 1989). Also, product content standards may not be met, such as with dyes and additives (Chute, 1990), or product content may be different from authorized goods and safe but yet unacceptable, such as when the content of gray market baby shampoo or tooth paste smells funny to consumers, thus reducing consumer confidence ("Gray Marketers," 1988). Consumers may feel that authorized firms do not honor warranties (Duhan and Sheffet, 1988; Howell et al., 1986; Weigand, 1991), such as is the case with IBM personal computers (Lozano, 1988). Consumers may even be faced with instruction manuals in the wrong language (Meyerowitz, 1986). Lastly, consumers may believe that authorized firms are devious in using the ends, e.g., the profit objective, to justify the means, e.g., unethical marketing practices.

The manufacturer may have to additionally invest in the goods and brand names to prevent more damage to them. Consumer suspicion about the higher prices of authorized goods (Cavusgil and Sikora, 1988) may require firms in the channel to more strongly justify selling the goods "bundled" with peripheral aspects. Thus, managing products and brand names, margins, costs, and product positioning based on price may become more difficult in the channel.

Consumer confidence in authorized goods and in the manufacturer and its intermediaries may diminish if gray marketing causes postpurchase dissatisfaction (Duhan and Sheffet, 1988; Howell et al., 1986; Ludwig and Koenig, 1990; Maskulka and Gulas, 1987). The dissatisfaction may affect repeat purchase behavior, brand loyalty, especially for brand name extensions, and may cause consumers to complain to the manufacturer, its retailers, or other consumers (Mowen, 1993; Peter and Olsen, 1993). Thus, gray marketing may hurt the manufacturer's future product offering and market entry, which may be costly to consumers and society.

Gray marketing presents perceived consumer risks—financial, performance, physical, psychological, and opportunity loss (Mowen, 1993; Peter and Olsen, 1993)—whose outcomes depend on consumer satisfaction with gray market goods. To willingly assume the risks and make intelligent decisions, consumers should know gray market goods exist and be able to easily identify them. This may be difficult, however, if retailers mix gray market goods and authorized goods together at the same price (Ludwig and Koenig, 1990), without consumer knowledge.

Outcomes are positive when consumers perceive gray market goods as satisfactory because they increase use of discretionary income, perform acceptably, operate safely, fit consumers' self-images, provide better product assortment, availability, and pricing, or sometimes offer higher quality than authorized goods (Commins, 1990). Outcomes are negative for unsatisfactory gray market goods that are: unsafe, unreliable, damaged, aged, obsolete, or not under warranty or service contract; overly-available; not supported by parts or inventories; accompanied by manuals in foreign languages or inadequate warnings; or not in the manufacturer's records since they were bought from unauthorized resellers, which may prevent consumer notification of product recalls (Duhan and Sheffet, 1988; Dwyer and Dunkin, 1988; Lozano, 1988; Ludwig and Koenig, 1990). Unsatisfactory gray market goods may: cost more in the long-run due to premature repair or replacement, perform unacceptably, cause safety hazards, diminish the value and image the trademarked brand name had conveyed and consumers had desired

(Cavusgil and Sikora, 1988; Maskulka and Gulas, 1987), or cause consumers to forego buying the authorized good.

Consumers who knowingly bought gray market goods and complain about dissatisfaction may behave unethically if they engaged in "consumer free-riding" (Mowen, 1993). In "consumer free-riding," the consumer uses full-service retailers in the search process to obtain product information and identify satisfactory alternatives, subsequently using the information to purchase from a low-cost retailer. It is common in gray market purchases, with the authorized retailers as full-service retailers and gray marketers as low-cost retailers.

To offset problems with consumers, the manufacturer and its intermediaries may use advertising or other means to educate consumers about gray marketing and its risks. To fulfill fiduciary responsibilities to consumers, firms in the channel should educate consumers about all perspectives of gray marketing in order for them to make intelligent purchase decisions. Educating consumers about gray marketing should involve consumers' basic rights regarding the marketing of products: the right to safety, to be informed, to choose, and to be heard.[6]

Gray marketing may make advertising less effective. Advertising for brand-named consumer goods that is used in "free-riding" is usually directly linked to the authorized goods, brand names, and firms in the channel and, thus, may damage their images and values. Unlike signals from communication firms, which have relatively clear legal protection, advertising has no definitive legal protection against unauthorized use, which is a great advantage to gray marketers. Firms may need to expand advertising, perhaps with disclaimers about gray marketing or statements that warranties will not cover gray market goods. However, if consumers do not believe that the risk outcomes would be negative, this may only serve to educate them about alternative sourcing.

Diverting may be reduced by changing ordering policies that do not allow intermediaries to change or cancel excessively large orders, or by changing price/quantity schedules so that smaller increments of product volume can be offered. In either case, the buyer has more flexibility in managing purchasing costs. This may appeal to business people from cultures where bargaining and negotiating are significant parts of the business culture and society in general if they perceive the transactions as thus fairer in both economic and ethical senses.

Reducing ethical risk to the salesforce from gray marketing should concern firms since, as stakeholders, they should basically be protected by management and not placed in situations that may cause conflicts in marketing ethics. Thus, management may need to examine sales management policies used to motivate that may cause conflict, such as sales quotas.

For the salesforce to understand the scope of the relationship of marketing ethics and gray marketing, management should educate them about the short and long-term effects of gray marketing, the use of policies to prevent it, and the consequences of involvement in it. Because the consequences of the sales person's behavior and performance level may affect how a sales manager actually disciplines the sales person for unethical behavior (DeConinck, 1992), firms should consider the sales manager's perceptions and judgments and the salesforce performance when using policies to prevent gray marketing. Further, management should recognize that cross-cultural aspects that affect sales people may cause conflicts in marketing ethics.

Generally, firms in the channel may be more vulnerable to gray marketing if channel control relies more on implicit than explicit contracts and if control is inadequate. The vulnerability may decrease with increased management awareness of gray marketing and general precautions against it. Further, intermediaries may feel that gray marketing may hurt the profitability of authorized goods and may decide to stop or limit sales. Thus, the manufacturer may have to reexamine intermediaries to better manage in an environment with gray marketing.

Reducing ethical risk to intermediaries from gray marketing should concern the manufacturer because, as stakeholders, intermediaries should not be placed in situations where they may be in an ethical dilemma. Management may need to reexamine sales policies used to motivate intermediaries that may be detrimental to their long-term interests. Further, management may need to determine if marketing ethics, given cross-cultural differences, and the risk of diverting are affected by relationships among firms in the channel in terms of length of the relationship, e.g., short-term versus long-term, degree of commitment, e.g., solely purchasing versus coordinating marketing strategies, and economic importance, e.g., cost, sales, and profit.

The risk of gray marketing may be reduced by improving channel control through better agreements and a greater focus on marketing ethics related to the channel. The legality of gray marketing may be better addressed in explicit contracts, but should at least be implied in implicit ones. The ethicality of gray marketing should be addressed in both explicit and implicit contracts, but the latter will probably have the greater use in delineating marketing ethics because of the need to more strongly enforce implicit contracts through marketing ethics.

Increasing ethical compatibility among firms in the channel may improve channel control and marketing ethics. However, increases in the number of relationships and variables in the channel, often due to channel and environmental complexities and cultural differences, make this difficult. Also, managing compatibility is affected by the dynamics of ethical standards that constantly change in and among firms and among situations (Ferrell and Gresham, 1985). Further, it may be difficult in industries where problems in the ethical climate cause unethical behavior on which the industries thrive, such as gray marketing (Honigsbaum, 1988; Tsalikis and Fritzsche, 1989).

Technology in the form of marketing information systems may be used by firms in the channel to monitor and enforce marketing ethics relative to gray marketing. These systems are used to examine activities in the channel and gray markets and are essential for tracking movements of gray markets to protect the authorized firm's long-term profitability (Cavusgil and Sikora, 1988).

Management Orientation

Management's orientation may play a significant role in the performance of the firm relative to marketing ethics and gray marketing. It may greatly affect decisions in marketing strategy.

Management may find itself forced to take unpleasant action to combat gray marketing, given the potential damage from gray marketing. For example, the manufacturer is frequently forced to offer free warranty service or honor rebates for gray market goods (Minehan, 1991).

The firm's ability to manage marketing ethics relative to gray marketing may improve through a stronger focus on societal marketing, which may allow it to more easily convey its concerns about gray marketing and the need for compatibility in marketing ethics. However, the meaning and relevancy of societal marketing to firms will be complicated by the uniqueness of societies represented in the channel. Societal marketing addresses concerns about stakeholders (Gandz and Hayes, 1988), recognizes that marketing strategy will affect, and be affected by, stakeholders, and reflects the firm's degree of social responsibility in its marketing strategies. It is often the focus for the manufacturer's ethical concerns about the effect of marketing strategies, including distribution (Abratt and Sachs, 1988). The marketing strategy of a socially responsible firm should allow consumers to make intelligent purchase decisions and should avoid causing societal problems (Abratt and Sachs, 1988), such as gray marketing.

Management's perceptions of each stakeholder group's appropriate weight on its decisions may complicate preventing gray marketing, especially when the relative importance of each group to management differs across cultures. Management is the pivotal stakeholder group (Dobson, 1990), perhaps followed by shareholders (Cooke, 1991). Management's objective, as the corporate objective, may be based on financial economics, basically wealth maximization, or business ethics, basically acting to meet needs through preferences subject to ethics (Dobson, 1990). Thus, management may put its own interests, and perhaps those of shareholders, above those of other stakeholders, and the basis of its objective may be unclear. Management's cross-cultural attitudes about stakeholders may suggest future problems in fighting gray marketing. For example, Becker and Fritzsche (1987) find that marketing managers in the U.S., France, and Germany only partly agree that management should focus not only on the interests of shareholders but also those of employees and consumers for management to behave ethically. This implies that these managers could have a low, if any, focus on being socially responsible to all stakeholders, which may cause problems in preventing gray marketing.

Management's interest in formally managing business ethics in general and marketing ethics in particular may significantly affect its ability to fight gray marketing. Ethical codes of conduct are used to reduce the opportunity for unethical behavior (Ferrell and Fraedrich, 1994), and, thus, may provide some means through which to combat gray marketing, depending on their explicitness and use within firms in the channel. Further, ethical ambivalence, as a form of social ambivalence, may exist within firms due to the conflict between the individual's ethical system and the firm's reward system (Jansen and Glinow, 1985). Ethical ambivalence may contribute to the potential for gray marketing, e.g., sales people may experience conflict between not meeting sales quotas and diverting. Firms should examine whether the ethical codes and reward systems can be effectively used, relative to their cross-cultural aspects, to prevent gray marketing.

Lastly, management's ability to analyze cross-cultural aspects that affect marketing ethics, and gray marketing may greatly depend on its understanding of the relevant cultures. To develop a better understanding of the values and ethics of business people, managers should thoroughly examine cultures, such as the degree to which they are high-context to low-context (Czinkota et al., 1993; Hall, 1989) and the part of culture for which information is easily acquired by outsiders, or frontstage culture, and the part of culture for which information is more restricted to outsiders, or backstage culture (Terpstra and David, 1991).

CONCLUSIONS

International gray marketing may result in negative outcomes that may be costly for consumers, firms in the channel, and society. Its legality and full degree of perceived ethicality should be examined to minimize these costs and to appropriately manage the channel within the environment. However, management of the channel relative to gray marketing becomes more difficult when cross-cultural aspects affect channel activities, marketing ethics, and gray marketing and when complexities of channel control and the environment increase.

Because of its lucrative nature, gray marketing will always exist somewhere in international marketing. Also, its locations for sourcing and selling may shift among markets and countries because of the characteristics, performance quality, and PLCs of potential gray market goods. Thus, cross-cultural aspects of marketing ethics and gray marketing will also change with gray market opportunities. Consequently, firms should have commensurate flexibility in their operations in order to effectively prevent gray marketing or to manage its effects.

Regarding future research, a contribution may be made by examining the cross-cultural marketing ethics of marketing managers in consumer goods industries and their attitudes toward gray marketing. Studies of the relationship of cross-cultural marketing ethics and the use of marketing agreements, i.e., explicit and implicit contracts, in the channel for consumer goods relative to gray marketing would also be interesting. Finally, investigations into marketing ethics within firms, e.g., ethical codes and ethical ambivalence, and between firms, e.g., ethical compatibility, relative to gray marketing may be of value.

AUTHOR NOTE

Lynette Knowles Mathur holds a PhD in International Business Marketing from Ohio State University. She lectures in marketing and international business at the undergraduate and MBA levels. Her publications are in the areas of international marketing, joint ventures, transfer pricing, and foreign exchange rate management, and she has contributed chapters and cases to several books. She is a member of the American Marketing Association, the Academy of Marketing Science, and the Academy of International Business. Her current research interests are associated with export marketing, joint ventures, international marketing, and distribution channels management. She has lived in Finland and has traveled extensively in Western Europe, Eastern (Central) Europe, North Africa, and China.

NOTES

1. Exceptions as to when gray marketing is illegal are presented later in this introduction. Gray market goods are not counterfeit goods, which are definitely illegal.

2. Gray market goods are also called "gray goods."

3. Fraudulent activities by gray marketers to obtain authorized goods may be illegal, but do not necessarily make the selling of the gray market goods obtained by fraud illegal.

4. The manufacturer is usually the owner of the trademark on the brand name (Minehan, 1991).

5. The gray market price is competitive, but is not a discount price. However, the lack of a discount retailer in an authorized channel may cause consumers to seek gray marketers.

6. These rights are part of the Consumer Bill of Rights issued in the early 1960s (see Peter and Olsen, 1993).

REFERENCES

Abratt, R., & Sacks, D. (1988). The marketing challenge: towards being profitable and socially responsible. *Journal of Business Ethics*, 7(7), 497-507.

Akaah, I. P. (1990). Attitudes of marketing professionals toward ethics in marketing research: A cross-national comparison. *Journal of Business Ethics*, 9(1), 45-53.

Akaah, I. P. (1992). Social inclusion as a marketing ethics correlate. *Journal of Business Ethics*, 11(8), 599-608.

Armstrong, L. (1988, March 14). Now Japan is feeling the heat from the gray market. *Business Week*, pp. 50-51.

Becker, H., & Fritzsche, D. J. (1987). Business ethics: A cross-cultural comparison of managers' attitudes. *Journal of Business Ethics*, 6(4), 289-295.

Cavusgil, S. T., & Sikora, E. (1988). How multinationals can counter gray market imports. *Columbia Journal of World Business*, 23(4) Winter, 75-85.

Cespedes, F. V., Corey, R., & Rangan, V. K. (1988). Gray markets: causes and cures. *Harvard Business Review*, 88(July-August), 75-82.

Chonko, L. B., & Hunt, S. D. (1985). Ethics and marketing management: An empirical examination. *Journal of Business Research*, 13(3), 339-359.

Chute, Elizabeth (1990, February 23). Gray market persists amid lax customs laws. *Women's Wear Daily*, p. C65.

Cianci, G. (1988, August). Skirmish won, gray market war continues. *Chain Store Age Executive*, pp. 60, 64.

Commins, K. (1990, May 9). South Koreans crack down on unauthorized Spam imports. *Journal of Commerce*, p. 5A(1).

Cooke, R. A. (1991). Danger signs of unethical behavior: How to determine if your firm is at ethical risk. *Journal of Business Ethics* 10(4), 249-253.

Cross, J., Stephans, J., & Benjamin, R. E. (1992). Gray markets: A legal review and public policy perspective. *Journal of Public Policy & Marketing*, 9, 183-194.

Czinkota, Michael R., Ilkka A. Ronkainen, and Michael H. Moffett (1994). *International Business*, New York: The Dryden Press.

DeConinck, J. B. (1992). How sales managers control unethical sales force behavior. *Journal of Business Ethics* 11(10), 789-798.

Dobson, J. (1990). Reconciling financial economics and business ethics. *Business & Professional Ethics Journal* 10(4), 23-42.

Duhan, D. F., & Sheffet, M. J. (1988). Gray markets and the legal status of parallel importation. *Journal of Marketing* 52(2), 75-83.

Dwyer, P., & Dunkin, A. (1988, June 13). A red-letter day for gray marketers. *Business Week*, p. 30.

Engardio, P., Fins, A., Baudoin, B., & Tell, L.J. (1988, November 7). There's nothing black-and-white about the gray market. *Business Week*, pp. 172-174.

Epstein, E. M. (1989). Business ethics, corporate good citizenship and the corporate social policy press: A view from the United States. *Journal of Business Ethics*, 8(8), 583-595.

Ferrell, O.C., & Fraedrich, John (1994). *Business Ethics*. Boston: Houghton Mifflin.

Ferrell, O. C., & Gresham, L. G. (1985). A contingency framework for understanding ethical decision making in marketing. *Journal of Marketing*, 49(2), 87-96.

Gandz, J., & Hayes, N. (1988). Teaching business ethics. *Journal of Business Ethics*, 7(9), 657-669.

Gannon, V. (1991, April 26). Hatch reintroduces a bill to ban gray market goods. *Women's Wear Daily*, p. 3.

Getz, K. A. (1990). International codes of conduct: An analysis of ethical reasoning. *Journal of Business Ethics*, 9(7), 567-577.

Gray marketers win a big one. (1988, August). *Sales and Marketing Management*, 27.

Hall, Edward T. (1989). *Beyond Culture*. New York: Doubleday.

Harris, Philip R., & Moran, Robert T. *Managing Cultural Differences*. Houston: Gulf Publishing Company.

Honigsbaum, M. (1988, August). Dollars and Scents. *The Washington Monthly*, pp. 16-19.

Howell, R. D., Britney, R., Kuzdrall, P. J., & Wilcox, J. B. (1986). Unauthorized channels of distribution: gray markets. *Industrial Marketing Management*, 15(2), 257-263.

Jansen, E., & Von Glinow, M. A. (1985). Ethical ambivalence and organizational reward systems. *Academy of Management Review* 10(4), 814-822.

Laczniak, Gene R., & Murphy, Patrick E. (1993). *Ethical Marketing Decisions: The Higher Road*. Boston: Allyn and Bacon.

Laczniak, G. R., & Murphy, P. E. (1991). Fostering ethical marketing decisions. *Journal of Business Ethics*, 10(4), 259-271.

Langlois, C. C., & Schlegelmilch, B. B. (1990). Do corporate codes of ethics reflect national character? Evidence from Europe and the United States. *Journal of International Business Studies*, 21(4), 519-539.

Lowe, Larry S., & Kevin F. McCrohan. (1989). Minimize the impact of the gray market. *Journal of Business Strategy*, 10(November-December), 47-50.

Lozano, E. (1988, March). Big Blue's gray market ethics. *Computerworld*, p. 95.

Ludwig, E. A., & Koenig, E. S. (1990, March). Importing a fraud: gray-market products. *USA Today*, pp. 26-28.

Lysonski, S. (1991). A cross-cultural comparison of the ethics of business students. *Journal of Business Ethics*, 10(2), 141-150.

Maskulka, J., & Gulas, C. S. (1987). The long-term dangers of gray-market sales. *Business*, 37(January/February/March), 25-31.

Meyerowitz, S. A. (1986, May). Neither black nor white, the gray market fight continues. *Business Marketing*, pp. 96+.

Minehan, L. G. (1991). The gray market: A call for greater protection of consumers and trademark owners. *University of Pennsylvania Journal of International Business Law*, 12(Fall), 457-476.

Mowen, J. C. (1993). *Consumer Behavior.* New York: Macmillan, 3rd ed.

Peter, J. P., & Olsen, J. C. (1993). *Consumer Behavior and Marketing Strategy.* Homewood, Illinois: Irwin, 3rd ed.

Raiborn, C. A., & Payne, D. (1990). Corporate codes of conduct: a collective conscience and continuum. *Journal of Business Ethics*, 9(11), 879-889.

Rosenbloom, Bert (1991). *Marketing Channels.* New York: The Dryden Press, 4th ed.

Serko, D. (1986, September). Singing the gray market blues. *American Import-Export Management*, pp. 29-30.

Terpstra, Vern, and Kenneth David. *The Cultural Environment of International Business.* Cincinnati, Ohio: South-Western.

Tsalikis, J., & Fritzsche, D. J. (1989). Business ethics: A literature review with a focus on marketing ethics. *Journal of Business Ethics*, 8(9), 695-743.

Weigand, R. E. (1991). Parallel import channels–options for preserving territorial integrity. *Columbia Journal of World Business* 26(1) Spring, 53-60.

Whipple, T. W., & Swords, D. F. (1992). Business ethics judgments: A cross-cultural comparison. *Journal of Business Ethics*, 11(9), 671-678.

White, L. P., & Rhodeback, M. J. (1992). Ethical dilemmas in organizational development: A cross-cultural analysis. *Journal of Business Ethics*, 11(9), 663-670.

Wines, W. A., & Napier, N. K. (1992). Toward an understanding of cross-cultural ethics: A tentative model. *Journal of Business Ethics* 11(9), 831-841.

Ethical Decision Making
in Turkish Sales Management

Arturo Z. Vásquez-Párraga
Ali Kara

SUMMARY. Both scholars and practitioners in the various business professions are becoming increasingly interested in knowing what determines managers to judge subordinates' behaviors as ethical or unethical, and what prompts them to either choose certain rewards or certain punishments to encourage or discourage, respectively, behaviors that are judged ethical or unethical. Traditionally, the study of organizational consequences of employees' behavior has gained importance in view of the fact that managerial decisions aimed at influencing subordinates' ethical conduct seem to be affected by the consideration of the consequences of such behavior for the company (utilitarian ethics). More recently, the perception that people act morally because of a prevailing moral commitment (deontological ethics) has gained some ground. Moreover, recent research findings show that deontological (moral) considerations prevail over teleological (consequential) considerations. Our study replicates this research in a different setting (Turkey) and expands the analysis to investigate the influence of socialization and cultural values in ethical decision making. More specifically, this study examines the role of socialization and the role of culture in shaping moral commitment.

Arturo Z. Vásquez-Párraga is Assistant Professor of Marketing, Florida International University and Ali Kara is Assistant Professor of Marketing, Penn State University at York.

[Haworth co-indexing entry note]: "Ethical Decision Making in Turkish Sales Management." Vásquez-Párraga, Arturo Z., and Ali Kara. Co-published simultaneously in the *Journal of Euromarketing* (International Business Press, an imprint of The Haworth Press, Inc.) Vol. 4, No. 2, 1995, pp. 61-86; and: *Ethical Issues in International Marketing* (ed: Nejdet Delener) International Business Press, an imprint of The Haworth Press, Inc., 1995, pp. 61-86. Multiple copies of this article/chapter may be purchased from The Haworth Document Delivery Center [1-800-3-HAWORTH; 9:00 a.m. - 5:00 p.m. (EST)].

INTRODUCTION

A recent study (Hunt and Vásquez-Párraga 1993) offers research findings in which the formation of managers' ethical judgments and their decision to intervene are not determined by either moral commitments alone as "pure" deontologists contend or action consequences alone as neoclassical economists postulate. Hunt and Vásquez-Párraga show empirically that: (1) ethical judgments are reached by undertaking both deontological and teleological evaluations, as predicted by the theory (Hunt and Vitell 1986), (2) deontological evaluations have more influence than teleological evaluations in the formation of ethical judgments, as hypothesized by (so called) moderate deontologists (Etzioni 1988), (3) the decision to reward (punish) a salesperson to encourage (discourage) ethical (unethical) behavior is determined by both ethical judgment and teleological evaluations, as predicted by the theory (Hunt and Vitell 1986), and (4) the decision to reward (punish) a salesperson to encourage (discourage) ethical (unethical) behavior is more strongly guided by ethical judgments than by teleological evaluations.

Following a similar approach, this study examines the competing roles of both deontological and teleological evaluations in shaping Turkish managers' ethical decision making. The decision making process is comprised of two steps: judgment formation and action intention. In addition to previous studies, this research examines the role of socialization and cultural values in both the deontological and teleological evaluations. The assumption underlying this examination is that both socialization and cultural values represent the social background of a person and that, therefore, they serve as a framework in which the formation of deontological and teleological evaluations take place.

Thus, this study aims at both reproducing the ethical decision process used by Turkish sales and marketing managers and explaining the role of socialization and cultural values in the formation of either the deontological or teleological considerations, or both.

ETHICAL DECISION MAKING

A general theory of marketing ethics focusses on the ethical decision making process in which ethical outcomes (ethical judgments and intentions to intervene) are determined by deontological and teleological considerations[1] (Hunt and Vitell 1986; Hunt and Vásquez-Párraga 1993). Consequently, research in this field tries to answer the following central questions: (1) what determines managers' ethical judgments, (2) what determines managers' intentions to intervene, and (3) what influences the determinant factors of the ethical decision process. Answers to the first and second questions help understanding the process of managers' ethical decision process. Answers to the last question help identifying and controlling the environmental influences of the process.

In relation to the question of what determines ethical judgments, empirical tests of the Hunt-Vitell model and other models (Ferrell and Gresham 1985; Ferrell, Gresham, and Fraedrich 1989) have shown that both deontological and teleological considerations are taken into account to arrive at an ethical judgment. Previous research (except for the recent study by Hunt and Vásquez-Párraga) has not been successful in determining if managers rely more on deontological or teleological considerations when forming their ethical judgments and deciding on their action intentions. Hunt and Vásquez-Párraga (1993) found that managers use far more deontological considerations than teleological ones when making ethical judgments and/or deciding to intervene. These findings are very important in view of the fact that, from a broader perspective, people either seek to maximize individual utilities and shape behavior accordingly (utilitarian ethics), or people act morally first, and then behave consistent with such morals (deontological ethics).

Neoclassical economists (including both ultra-rationalists and moderate rationalists–see Etzioni 1988), a stream of utilitarians, assume that people rationally pursue the most efficient means to their goals, e.g., the most efficient allocation of resources in order to satisfy their wants (Browning and Browning 1983). Within such a framework, there is no distinction between ethical decisions and other decisions, or between moral values and other sources of valuation; all belong to the same bundle of preferences or the all-encompassing pleasure utility (McPherson 1984). Neoclassical economists not only ignore a distinctive moral dimension in human behavior, they oppose its inclusion as a separate source of valuation. They stress that various individuals may have different rankings of preferences over a field of choice, but none can be deemed to be better; all preferences including the preference of others encompass one utility, the individual's pleasure or interests. And pleasure is judged by its consequences.

Conversely, deontologists postulate that moral acts are a source of value other than pleasure (moral action is a matter of principles, whereas pleasure is a matter of consequences) and, thus, cannot be included among the pleasure utilities (Etzioni 1988). Deontologists distinguish between moral acts and other acts, and postulate that actions are morally right when they conform to a relevant principle or duty (the Greek *deon* means binding duty). A principle or criterion is internalized and used for judging the morality of an act, not the consequences it aspires to achieve (the way utilitarians believe). Value internalization, a distinctive feature of moral acts, marks a major difference between neoclassical psychologies that deny any type of internalization and deontological psychologies that recognize it. For deontologists, an internalized predisposition, when present, is guided by people's own inner values (duties), not by external constraints or environmental forces. Conversely, external constraints prevail when internalized values are absent or slack (Etzioni 1975). In reality, people internalize values and, thus, express commitments or intentions, which in turn become a cause that in part explains behavior (Fried 1964). As Hoffman (1985) points out, once internalization has taken place, people pursue what they consider to be a moral line of behavior, even in the absence of external sanctions.

In relation to the question of what determines managers' intentions to intervene in subordinates' ethical behavior, research has been scarce and limited. Management intervention to influence subordinates' behavior has been widely recognized to be the main constraint of work outcomes in general (Podsakoff 1982; Schoorman and Schneider 1988), and ethical behavior in particular (Posner and Schmidt 1987). More specifically, the use of leadership methods and some organizational means have often been recommended to discourage subordinates' unethical behavior or to encourage their ethical conduct.

Nevertheless, there is a recognition among marketers that the effectiveness of such usage has been limited, particularly in the use of codes of ethics. According to some, these codes did not adequately address all the major ethical problems of the target group (Hunt, Chonko, and Wilcox 1984; Chonko and Hunt 1985), or they often put too much of the burden to be ethical on employees, while ignoring ways in which companies can create an environment that facilitates employees' ethical conduct (Bingham and Raffield 1989). According to others, codes were insufficient to convince employees of the advantages of abiding by them (Laczniak and Inderrieden 1987), or they were not enforced or accompanied by adequate corporate policies on ethics (Murphy and Laczniak 1981). In addition, some authors noted that the majority of ethics policy statements have not addressed various important aspects of employees' ethical behavior (Hite, Bellizi, and Fraser 1988).

Thus, how to enforce codes of ethics and what to include in ethics policies? One alternative has been to use rewards and/or punishment systems (Ferrell and Gresham 1985; Bingham and Raffield 1989). However, empirical research has been limited to the use of punishment and the organizational and personal conditions under which punishment may operate. Bellizi and Hite (1989) used an experimental design to investigate the influence of negative organizational consequences (and two other factors) on management disciplinary actions and found that supervisory reaction is more severe when a negative consequence is stated than when no stated consequence is given. Using four scenarios representing ethical issues, Bellizi and Hite (1989) observed that sales managers are more likely to use more severe disciplinary measures when negative consequences, poor performers, and salesmen (as opposed to saleswomen) are involved in unethical selling behavior. The influence of gender on managers' reactions was replicated and the effects of obesity were investigated by Bellizi and Norvell (1991). Although limited in scope, this finding shows the importance of a teleological consideration for intentions to intervene in subordinates' behavior. Yet, Bellizi and Hite do not address the relative importance of such considerations versus other considerations (e.g., deontological ones) nor the effects of positive organizational consequences on intentions to intervene.

In relation to the question of what influences the determining factors of the ethical decision process, a discussion of the role of socialization and cultural values in ethical decision making follows.

SOCIALIZATION AND CULTURAL VALUES

The greater importance of deontological considerations as compared to the importance of teleological considerations in both the formation of ethical judgments and the decision to either reward an ethical behavior or punish an unethical one prompts the question of what influences deontological evaluations or what shapes moral commitment, a core deontological consideration (Etzioni 1988). Moral commitment seems to be rooted in the cultural background of the individual. That is, individuals see values (e.g., duties) as part of their personality, not as external conditions to which they merely adapt (e.g., pleasurable consequences). People seem to persevere out of a strong sense that they ought to, "that it is the right thing to do" although not, by and large, an enjoyable one.

Moreover, what distinguishes moral commitments from other acts is their sense of value, and values are internalized. Internalization has been defined as part of the socialization process in which a person learns to "conform to rules in situations that arouse impulses to transgress and that lack surveillance and sanctions" (Kohlberg 1981). The process of socialization, in which a child becomes an autonomous person, is largely one of internalization of values, of building up self-control rather than control by external forces (Etzioni 1988). Once internalization has taken place, individuals pursue what they consider to be a moral line of behavior even in the absence of external sanctions (Hoffman 1983). Hence, the behavior of properly socialized adults is deeply influenced by their absolute morality, aside from whatever expedient effects it has.

Research may trace the origins of one's moral commitments to one's parents, grandparents, relatives, peer or reference groups; but whatever their source, once internalized, they become an integral part of the self. Both length and strength of the socialization process are of paramount importance to internalization.

In addition, research may account for perceptual differences due to differences in cultural values. For instance, some managers may value honesty more than profits because of pro-active religious beliefs, while some others may value monetary rewards more than being on an honor roll because of a cultural preference for immediate gratification. Identification of one's cultural values can help explain the nature of the differences between a group's deontological evaluations vs. another group's deontological evaluations.

Thus, research on people's socialization and cultural values is of great importance to the study of business decision-making involving ethical content mainly because of two reasons. First, it helps understand how deontological evaluations are developed. Second, it helps explain variances in the formation of deontological evaluations, assuming that a substantial portion of such variances can be explained by cultural differences.

Furthermore, a current problem in cross-cultural research on ethics is the substitution of the person's culture by the person's nationality, and thus the treatment of culture as a residual variable (Ronen 1986). Such treatment may bias the interpretation of differences between groups that belong to different countries. The usual conclusion that two groups are different because they belong to different countries is of great concern in cross-cultural research, more so when the topic of research has to do with culture as in the case of ethics.

For instance, Burns and Brady (1991) recently concluded that "American students possess 'more ethical' perceptions than Malaysian students," and that –as suggested previously by Thorelli (cited by Burns and Brady)–" 'lower' ethical perceptions can be expected among individuals in a developing country than those in a developed country." The fact that these Malaysian students obtained a lower score than their American counterparts can neither be attributed to nor explained by their nationality (in substitution of cultural differences). Good research has to escape the "residual definition" of culture and examine culture or a cultural manifestation empirically if it is going to be used to explain outcomes.

HYPOTHESES

Figure 1 shows the variables and relationships that are included in this study. Hypotheses 1 and 2 aim at replicating Hunt and Vásquez-Párraga's (1993) findings in a new context, Turkish sales and marketing managers.

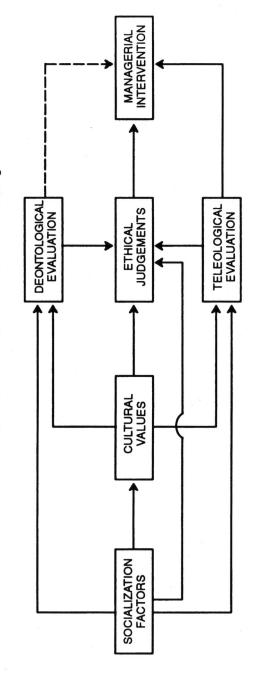

FIGURE 1. Model of Cross-Cultural Ethical Decision Making.

H1: Turkish sales and marketing managers use both deontological and teleological evaluations to both form ethical judgments and adopt a decision to either reward or punish the salesperson to either encourage ethical behavior or discourage unethical behavior, respectively.

H2: Deontological evaluations have more influence than teleological evaluations in both the formation of ethical judgments by Turkish managers and their decision to intervene.

Hypotheses 3, 4, 5 and 6 expand previous research to include the examination of the influences of socialization and cultural values in both the deontological and teleological evaluations.

H3: The longer and stronger is the managers' socialization process, the greater the effects of deontological considerations on both their ethical judgments and their decision to intervene, as compared to the effects of teleological considerations on the same outcomes.

H4: The longer and stronger is the managers' socialization process, the greater the effects of ethical judgments on their decision to intervene, as compared to the effects of teleological considerations on the same outcome.

H5: The stronger is the cultural-value identification of the manager, the greater the effects of deontological considerations on both their ethical judgments and their decision to intervene, as compared to the effects of teleological considerations on the same outcomes.

H6: The stronger is the cultural-value identification of the manager, the greater the effects of ethical judgments on their decision to intervene, as compared to the effects of teleological considerations on the same outcome.

METHODOLOGY

Research Design

This study is based on a completely randomized design. An experimental design enables the primary sources of variability to be identified and the amount of variability due to each source to be separated out of the total variability in the data (Kirk 1982). In a completely randomized design, the experimental units are randomly assigned to k treatments, in this case four treatment groups: the four cells resulting from the combination of two deontological conditions (ethical and unethical) with two teleological conditions (positive and negative organizational consequences).

Eight selling scenarios were developed, two for each treatment group. Scenarios are the primary ethics research method and can be fruitfully used when the ethical issues that underlie them are systematically manipulated (Alexander and Becker 1978; Hunt, Chonko, and Wilcox 1984), or when researchers want to generate large differences among respondents on the "ethical judgments" issue (Hunt 1990). Each scenario reflected a combination of a deontological condition with a teleological condition, maintaining every other condition fixed. Both the content of the scenarios and the mode of utilizing them were taken from Hunt and Vásquez-Párraga (1993).

Two representations of (un)ethical problems were chosen for the scenarios: overstating plant capacity utilization and over-recommending expensive products of the firm. Overstating plant capacity utilization is an attempt to convey favorable demand conditions by suggesting product popularity to customers and by discouraging, as a result, price negotiations on the part of the buyer. Such an attempt involves lying to the customer and violates the "truth telling" deontological norm. Over-recommending expensive products of the company is an attempt to build the dollar size of an order to perhaps earn higher commissions by selling a customer higher quality than is actually needed. Such an attempt involves deceiving the customer and violates the deontological norm of "trust." Both norms, "truth telling" and "trust," are considered universal norms (Kohlberg 1981) and, thus, feasibly evaluated across cultures and countries.

A pre-test of 30 respondents showed that Turkish managers were familiar with these scenarios, that the scenarios were not culture-bound, and that using the same scenarios would allow for comparison across samples. Moreover, Turkish managers preferred to answer using the English version of the questionnaire, enhancing the comparability of samples.

Because each questionnaire presented two scenarios, subjects were instructed to read each scenario separately and to answer the questions about their ethical judgment and intentions to intervene in relation to that scenario only. The addition of a second scenario proved to be a useful strategy not only because it stimulated the respondent with a different theme, and it facilitated the discovery of method artifacts in the issues involved, but also because it served as a replication test of the measures with exactly the same sample.

Measurement

The two dependent variables, ethical judgment and managerial intervention, were measured by scales specifically developed and shown to be valid and reliable measures by Hunt and Vásquez-Párraga (1993). Both measures were replicated identically in the Turkish sample. Ethical judgment was measured on a 7-point Likert scale from 1 = very unethical to 4 = neither ethical nor unethical to 7 = very ethical. Managerial intervention (reward or punishment) was initially measured by a scale from 1 = termination of employment to 5 = no action at all to 9 = pay raise and promotion. A metric of the intervention scale from − 10 to +10 was used to test for nomological validity of the scale. Following the procedures suggested by Rossi, Wright, and Anderson (1983), the scale was tested valid in both contexts, American and Turkish. Moreover, both scales in the Turkish sample relate to other variables (deontological and teleological evaluations) in the same direction and similar strength the scale relates to same variables in the American sample.

The length and strength of the process of socialization of the individual were captured by number of years the interviewee lived with parents, grandparents, brothers and sisters, children, and other relatives. The presence and strength of the person's cultural values were measured by 10 scales specifically designed for this research.

Sample

Sales and marketing managers are the subjects of study. At this level of managerial responsibility the effects of both ethical judgments and management actions (rewards or punishment) could be properly evaluated mainly because situational constraints tend to have relatively uniform effects on individuals when they all share a common work environment, either due to the homogenizing conditions of work climates (Schneider and Reichers 1983), or as a result of an organizational culture in place (Schein 1985).

The sampling frame used was a large national base of sales and marketing executives available in Turkey. First, a list of the Fortune-like 500 companies was used. Because of this list overrepresenting the larger companies, a list of 195 small companies supplied to us by the Istanbul Chamber of Commerce was added. The total list of 695 was used as a sample, after pretesting a probable response rate of 20%. After discounting for undeliverable questionnaires (21) and incomplete returns (29), and including the responses to the short form containing demographic information (32), the effective response rate was 22.6%. The results reported here are based on 114 complete and usable returns.

A short form with only demographic information was used to examine the issue of non-response bias. T-tests and chi square tests resulted in no significant differences on the demographic profiles of both samples. Similarly, there are no differences between the first and the second wave of respondents. Finally, the four experimental groups are demographically identical.

Among the respondents, two thirds are in top positions in the company, including some in top management. There are more sales managers than marketing managers, but some sales managers also perform marketing functions. Sales and marketing managers are principally male, middle-aged, with some (but not too many) years of experience, relatively high income, and relatively high levels of education. Two thirds are from Istanbul, the largest city, where industries concentrate, but one third represent 17 other cities of the country. The 3 economic sectors are proportionately represented and include the 24 industries that account for approximately 90% of economic activity of the country. As professional background, 48% of managers have engineering background, and 44% business background; 85% work for a private company, whereas 15% work for a public company. We should also note that 100% of the sample is Turkish (as ethnic background), 97% is Moslem, 97% speak Turkish at home, 70% speak Turkish at work, and 30% speak English and/or German at work.

Questionnaire

Data were gathered by a self-administered pretested questionnaire (four versions) randomly distributed and mailed to a national sample of sales and marketing managers. Both an English version and a Turkish version of the questionnaire were included in the mailing. The Turkish version followed a process of double-back translation to ensure construct validity. Moreover, two out of three respondents preferred the English version, minimizing the problems attached to translation. Similarly, a letter of presentation and the short form were included in both languages. Finally, a self-addressed return envelope was also provided.

Statistical Methods

Both multiple correlations and regression analysis were applied to the combined sample (where the two cases are merged) in order to test the hypotheses. Table 1 reports the means and standard deviations of the core independent and dependent variables. The socialization and culture-related variables are examined through the interaction terms between each of these variables and the core independent variables as follows: deontological and teleological evaluations when related to ethical judgments, and both evaluations and ethical judgments when related to the decision to intervene.

RESULTS AND DISCUSSION

An examination of the correlation matrix (Table 1) shows that both deontological and teleological considerations are strongly correlated to both ethical judgments and managerial intervention, and, hence, neither reductionism to moral commitment nor reductionism to consequences (a long-time held utilitarian perspective of decision-making on matters that involve ethical content) reflect the actual process used by business decision-makers. In addition, Tables 2 and 3 show the basic model main effects. All relationships are significant at $p < .0001$, except for the effects of teleological evaluations on ethical judgment which are significant at $p < .05$, and the effects of deontological evaluations on intervention. According

TABLE 1. Correlation Matrix.

	Mean	Std. Dev.	Deontological evaluation	Teleological evaluation	Ethical judgment
Deontological Evaluation	1.438	0.497			
Teleological Evaluation	1.473	0.500	−0.024		
Ethical Judgment	4.285	2.116	0.752**	0.138*	
Managerial Intervention	5.265	1.971	0.546**	0.368**	0.754**

* significant at $p < .05$
** significant at $p < .0001$

to the theory (Hunt and Vitell 1986), deontological evaluations should not have a direct impact on INTERVENTION. Our findings corroborate the theory. Thus, Hypothesis 1 was corroborated.

Moreover, the correlation matrix also shows that the deontological considerations have a greater effect than the teleological considerations on both how Turkish managers form their ethical judgments (.75 vs. .14) and how they decide to intervene in a salesperson's ethical behavior (.54 vs. .37). Hypothesis 2 was also corroborated.

Overall, the above tests confirm (1) the relative importance of both deontological and teleological considerations in forming ethical judgments, (2) the prevalence of the deontological considerations over the teleological ones in explaining the variance of ethical judgments, and (3) the impact of teleological considerations and ethical judgments on the decision to reward or punish when taking a managerial action.

Hypothesis 3 examines the influence of the length of the socialization process in deontological evaluations vs. the influence of such process in teleological evaluations. Table 2 shows the regression results for the various models to be compared. Only the ethical judgment models that include the socialization variables explain a slightly greater percentage of the variance in the dependent variable than the basic model. No socialization variable interacts with deontological evaluations in either its relationship with ethical judgment or its relationship with managerial intervention.

Conversely, some socialization variables significantly interact with teleological evaluations when explaining the formation of ethical judgments. Meaningfully, the length of socialization with parents and that with relatives significantly affect the respondent's teleological evaluations. Thus, Hypothesis 3 was rejected. Alternatively, socialization with parents and relatives influence teleological evaluations (not deontological evaluations), although the consequence of such interaction does not increase the explanatory power of teleological evaluations over that of deontological evaluations.

Understanding why socialization interacts with teleological evaluations (not with deontological evaluations) may take further analysis, preferably in the context of cross-cultural research. At this point, we can suspect that socialization in Turkey is more outcome-based than behavior-based, and that parents and relatives in charge of education are more inclined to teach the goodness and badness of human actions than to teach the rightness and/or wrongness of them.

In relation to Hypothesis 4, socialization with parents significantly interacts with ethical judgments when this variable relates to managerial intervention. It does not increase, however, the explained variance in the dependent variable. Hypothesis 4 was corroborated regarding one socialization factor. Four others showed no impact on the dependent variable.

Hypothesis 5 examines the influence of the cultural-value identification of the interviewee in both types of evaluations. Table 3 shows the regression results for the various models to be compared. The five models with the cultural-value variables present explain a slightly greater percentage of the variance in the dependent variable than the basic model. Four models include at least one significant interaction between a cultural-value variable and a core independent variable. Yet, the largest number of interactions occur with teleological evaluations. Only two cultural values, the emphasis on spiritual values and a preference for home socialization significantly interact with deontological evaluations. Thus, Hypothesis 5 is weakly corroborated. Alternatively, several cultural values influence teleological evaluations when both forming an ethical judg-

TABLE 2. Socialization Factors: Regression Results.

	Dependent Variables							
	Ethical Judgment				Managerial Intervention			
	Parameter (understandardized)	t	p <	R²	Parameter (understandardized)	t	p <	R²
CORE RELATIONSHIPS								
INTERCEPT	-1.295	-3.29	0.00	.59	0.643	1.83	0.07	.65
DEON	3.216	17.44	0.00		0.132	0.53	0.60	
TELEO	0.645	3.52	0.00		1.120	6.80	0.00	
ETHIC	.				0.644	10.91	0.00	
DEONTOLOGICAL EVALUATIONS								
INTERCEPT	-0.458	-3.56	0.00	.60	0.576	1.56	0.12	.65
DEON	-3.082	3.57	0.00		0.244	0.32	0.75	
TELEO	0.698	3.70	0.00		1.130	6.66	0.00	
ETHIC	.				0.637	10.68	0.00	
DEON × With parents	-0.168	-1.29	0.19		-0.143	-1.26	0.21	
DEON × With grandparents	-0.107	0.60	0.54		0.121	0.78	0.43	
DEON × With siblings	0.007	0.06	0.96		0.107	0.97	0.33	
DEON × With children	-0.027	-0.20	0.84		-0.082	-0.71	0.48	
DEON × With relatives	0.364	1.11	0.27		-0.082	-0.29	0.77	

76

TELEOLOGICAL EVALUATIONS

		.6 1				.6 5	
INTERCEPT	−1.579	−3.93	0.00	0.616	1.66	0.09
DEON	3.369	17.71	0.00	0.156	0.59	0.55
TELEO	0.059	0.08	0.94	1.795	2.67	0.00
ETHIC				0.644	10.62	0.00
TELEO × With parents	−0.215	−1.75	0.08	−0.106	−0.96	0.34
TELEO × With grandparents	0.091	0.54	0.59	0.024	−0.16	0.87
TELEO × With siblings	0.137	1.03	0.30	0.082	0.70	0.49
TELEO × With children	−0.049	−0.38	0.70	−0.115	−1.01	0.31
TELEO × With relatives	0.664	2.39	0.02	−0.232	−0.93	0.35

ETHICAL JUDGMENTS

					.6 5	
INTERCEPT				0.588	1.61	0.11
DEON				0.197	0.75	0.45
TELEO				1.120	6.67	0.00
ETHIC				0.761	3.20	0.00
ETHIC × With parents				−0.058	−1.63	0.10
ETHIC × With grandparents				0.036	0.72	0.47
ETHIC × With siblings				0.047	1.30	0.19
ETHIC × With children				−0.038	−1.05	0.29
ETHIC × With relatives				−0.092	−1.12	0.26

TABLE 3. Cultural Values: Regression Results.

| | Dependent Variables | | | | | | | |
| | Ethical Judgment | | | | Managerial Intervention | | | |
	Parameter (understandardized)	t	p <	R²	Parameter (understandardized)	t	p <	R²
CORE RELATIONSHIPS				.59				.65
INTERCEPT	-1.295	-3.29	0.00		0.643	1.83	0.07	
DEON	3.216	17.44	0.00		0.132	0.53	0.60	
TELEO	0.645	3.52	0.00		1.120	6.80	0.00	
ETHIC					0.644	10.91	0.00	
DEONTOLOGICAL EVALUATIONS				.62				.66
INTERCEPT	-1.328	-3.14	0.00		1.042	2.76	0.00	
DEON	2.781	5.12	0.00		-0.214	-0.41	0.67	
TELEO	0.528	2.27	0.00		1.019	5.84	0.00	
ETHIC					0.638	10.53	0.00	
DEON × Home-socialization	-0.033	-0.90	0.37		-0.051	-1.62	0.10	
DEON × Business	-0.048	-1.36	0.17		0.023	0.77	0.44	
DEON × Mosque/Church	-0.028	-0.73	0.46		-0.050	-1.44	0.15	
DEON × Family values	-0.002	-0.05	70.96		0.034	0.92	0.36	
DEON × Hiring criteria	0.056	1.33	0.18		0.039	1.05	0.29	
DEON × Spiritual values	0.081	1.79	0.08		0.018	0.46	0.65	
DEON × Honesty	0.014	0.27	0.79		-0.015	-0.34	0.73	
DEON × Religious	0.066	1.60	0.11		0.056	1.44	0.15	

TELEOLOGICAL EVALUATIONS

	b	t	p	b	t	p
INTERCEPT	-1.231	-2.91	0.00	1.147	3.13	0.00
DEON	3.143	15.92	0.00	-0.006	-0.02	0.98
TELEO	-0.150	-0.27	0.79	0.542	1.15	0.25
ETHIC				0.623	10.49	0.00
TELEO × Home-socialization	-0.033	-0.90	0.37	-0.060	-1.90	0.06
TELEO × Business	-0.010	-0.29	0.77	0.023	0.77	0.44
TELEO × Mosque/Church	-0.016	-0.44	0.65	-0.072	-2.31	0.02
TELEO × Family values	-0.012	-0.32	0.75	0.072	2.23	0.03
TELEO × Hiring criteria	0.075	1.73	0.09	0.093	2.50	0.01
TELEO × Spiritual values	0.101	2.47	0.01	0.009	0.24	0.80
TELEO × Honesty	0.006	0.11	0.91	-0.015	-0.33	0.74
TELEO × Religious	0.070	1.72	0.09	0.053	1.51	0.13

.61 .68

ETHICAL JUDGMENTS

	b	t	p
INTERCEPT	0.971	2.60	0.01
DEON	0.031	0.12	0.90
TELEO	1.032	5.95	0.00
ETHIC	0.525	3.46	0.00
ETHIC × Home-socialization	-0.013	-1.41	0.16
ETHIC × Business	0.003	0.26	0.79
ETHIC × Mosque/Church	-0.013	-1.22	0.22
ETHIC × Family values	0.014	1.25	0.21
ETHIC × Hiring criteria	0.014	1.20	0.23
ETHIC × Spiritual values	0.004	0.29	0.77
ETHIC × Honesty	-0.000	-0.03	0.98
ETHIC × Religious	0.019	1.53	0.13

.66

ment and making a decision. Three out of eight interaction terms with teleological evaluations are significant when explaining ethical judgments, and four out of eight, when explaining managerial intervention.

The preference for trust and cultural similarity over technical and professional qualifications to hire an employee on behalf of the company has significant interaction with teleological evaluations when explaining both ethical judgments and managerial intervention. Similarly, the social preference for childhood socialization at home under parents' guidance over school or university socialization also interacts significantly with teleological evaluations when explaining both outcomes. In other significant interactions with teleological evaluations, (1) family values are preferred over other types of values when solving life problems, (2) membership in a mosque or religion is considered highly desirable, (3) spiritual values are considered more important than material things, and (4) religious practice and active participation in religious events are also valued highly.

In relation to Hypothesis 6, there is no significant interaction between cultural values and ethical judgments when this variable relates to managerial intervention. Hypothesis 6 was rejected.

CONCLUSIONS AND MANAGERIAL IMPLICATIONS

This study discussed a relevant issue for both marketing scholars and practitioners by providing an empirical corroboration and a meaningful extension of a previously formulated theory of marketing ethics. The fundamental thrust of the research is that the formation of ethical judgments and the generation of intentions to managerially intervene are not determined by either moral commitments alone or action consequences alone, as either "pure" deontologists or neoclassical economists postulate, respectively. This research shows that neither reductionism to moral commitment nor reductionism to consequences (a long-time held utilitarian perspective of decision-making on matters that involve ethical content) reflect the actual process used by sales and marketing managers. It shows that both moral commitment and organizational consequences determine ethical judgments and the decision to intervene. Furthermore, it shows that moral commitment has a greater influence on the formation of managers' ethical judgments and their decision to intervene than organizational consequences do.

The validation and extension of a tested theory (Hunt and Vitell 1986; Hunt and Vásquez-Párraga 1993) through data and procedures used in this research signifies at least two primary contributions. First, we can better understand the process of decision-making in areas that involve ethical concerns by empirically corroborating a theory, helping develop law-like generalizations (Hunt 1991), and by expanding an existing theory through incorporating an examination of the influence of socialization and cultural values in ethical decision making. The use of a Turkish sample makes this validation and extension even more useful, particularly for international marketers.

This study demonstrates that: (1) ethical judgments are reached by undertaking both deontological and teleological evaluations, as predicted by the theory (Hunt and Vitell 1986), (2) deontological evaluations have more influence than teleological evaluations to both reach an ethical judgment and take a decision to intervene, as shown in the total effects of both independent variables on both dependent variables, and as hypothesized by (so called) moderate deontologists (Etzioni 1988), (3) socialization influences teleological evaluations more than deontological evaluations when these evaluations are used to form ethical judgments. It influences ethical judgments more than teleological evaluations when both are used to arrive at a decision to intervene, and (4) cultural values influence both deontological and teleological evaluations when evaluations are used to form ethical judgments and arrive at decisions to intervene. Their influence on teleological evaluations is, however, greater than that on deontological evaluations.

The managerial consequences of these findings are paramount. A current concern is how to influence subordinates' behavior that involves ethical issues. The classical remedy of providing norms (such as codes of ethics) alone underscored the importance of deontological considerations in action-taking. But codes of ethics have not worked (Laczniak and Inderrieden 1987; Ferrell and Fraedrich 1988; Bingham and Raffield 1989), showing that the provision of norms alone may not yield managerial expected results.

Such a failure may also imply that the assumed linkage between deontological considerations and managerial actions is not explicit but implicit. Comparing the correlation matrix and the regression results, we can see that the relationship is implicit indeed, as deontological considerations do not affect intervention directly but indirectly. Such an effect is, nevertheless, stronger than all the other effects taken together.

In contrast, teleological considerations affect intervention both directly and indirectly (through their influence on ethical judgments). Accordingly, managers may seem to pay less attention to norms and more attention to the positive or negative consequences of subordinates' behavior for the company when they have to decide the course of action through rewards or punishment that seek to influence subordinates' behavior. In fact, however, managers pay less attention to norms that may have less of an impact on the ethical judgments, and more attention to both norms that are influential and the consequences that can be produced by the performed behavior. In turn, ethical judgments directly and powerfully determine the manager's decision to reward or punish to either encourage ethical behavior or discourage unethical conduct, respectively.

STUDY LIMITATIONS

There are some limitations of this study. Three of them are of particular concern for the reviewers: the replication of a study done in the U.S. in a Turkish environment, the issues of internal and external validity, and the explanatory power of the socialization and cultural factors.

First, this is a replication and extension of a study done in a different social context and it legitimately raises the question of environmental appropriateness to either replicate scenarios or analyze similar relationships. A pre-test gave us an indication of appropriateness for the use of these scenarios. Other scenarios, however, may not be as "universal" as these and require content adaptations. The tested relationships among the core variables are symmetrical in both samples and, thus, provide similar corroborations of the same theory. The impact of the environmental variables (socialization and cultural values), however, is relatively weak and needs further research.

Second, although the fundamental issues of internal and external validity are explicitly addressed in the text (methodology), some other issues, such as demand artifacts in the Turkish environment, were not confronted. In the American sample, the impact of demand artifacts was minimized through random assignment of respondents to treatment conditions. Similarly, in the Turkish sample, the assignment was random but the sample is smaller and there is a potential nonresponse bias as in most ethics research.

Finally, the relatively weak explanatory power of the chosen environmental factors, socialization and cultural values, brings the question of how appropriate is this exploration to better understanding the formation of both deontological and teleological evaluations. Although the results are not decisive at this point, the exclusion of such variables in future research can be premature and theoretically unsound. Further exploration is needed in both similar and different social contexts before a decision is taken on the explanatory value of these environmental factors.

AUTHOR NOTES

Dr. Arturo Z. Vásquez-Párraga joined the faculty of the Department of Marketing and Environment of Florida International University (FIU) as Assistant Professor in August, 1990. He has a BA (1981) from the Catholic University of Peru, an MA (1983) and a PhD (1986) in Demography and Economics from the University of Texas at Austin, and a second PhD (1990) in Marketing and International Business from Texas Tech University.

Dr. Vásquez is an experienced international researcher in the areas of marketing research, business ethics, and labor research. His current areas of interest include international business strategy, export decision factors, consumer decision making, cross-cultural business ethics, travel marketing, and Hispanic marketing. He has published in leading American journals such as the *Journal of Marketing Research* and world-wide known publications such as the *International Labor Organization Working Papers*.

In the area of professional continuing education, he has trained scholars in international institutions such as the Instituto Tecnologico y de Estudios Superiores de Monterrey (ITESM) in Mexico City, and the American Graduate School of International Management (AGSIM)-Thunderbird in Glendale, Arizona.

As a consultant, Dr. Vásquez has worked for Volume Shoe Corporation (Chicago), Publicidad Siboney (Chicago), Coe and Company, Inc. (New York), Abbott

Laboratories (Chicago), Pitman and Moore (Miami), and the Andean Pact (Lima, Peru). On behalf of the Center for International Business Environment Studies (CIBES) at FIU, he has produced professional reports for Coca-Cola Company, American Express, Black and Decker, McDonald's Corporation, and Eastman Kodak Company. He has been very active in professional community services including speeches at conferences, roundtables, workshops, and TV programs.

Ali Kara holds a PhD in marketing from Florida International University. He received his Master of Business Administration (MBA) degree from the University of Bridgeport, Bridgeport, Connecticut and a second MBA degree from Cukurova University, Adana, Turkey. He has a Bachelor of Arts (BA) degree from Cukurova University, Adana, Turkey.

Dr. Kara's current research interests include Modelling Consumer Choices, Conjoint Analysis, improving the Adaptive Analytic Hierarchy Process (AHP) for marketing problems, testing the performances of existing decision making models, market segmentation and cluster analysis. His articles appear in publications such as *Journal of Advertising, Journal of Global Marketing*, and *The International Journal of Management Science: Omega*. He also has several national and international conference papers/presentations. He is a member of the American Marketing Association and the Academy of Marketing Science.

NOTE

1. Deontological considerations focus on the specific actions or behaviors of an individual, whereas teleological considerations focus on the consequences of the actions or behaviors. For deontologists, people have certain "prima facie" (at first sight) duties which, under most circumstances, constitute moral obligations (Ross 1930). For teleologists, people determine the consequences of various behaviors in a situation and evaluate the goodness or badness of all the consequences (Harris 1986). For utilitarians, a stream of teleologists, people evaluate the consequences for all people, not just the consequences for an individual (or as Frankena (1973) stated: "the greatest good for the greatest number").

REFERENCES

Alexander, Cheryl S., and Henry Jay Becker (1978), "The Use of Vignettes in Survey Research," *The Public Opinion Quarterly,* 42, 1 (Spring), 93-104.

Anderson, Erin and Richard L. Oliver (1987), "Perspectives on Behavior-Based versus Outcome-Based Salesforce Control Systems," *Journal of Marketing,* 51, 4 (October), 76-88.

Bellizi, Joseph A. and Robert E. Hite (1989), "Supervising Unethical Salesforce Behavior," *Journal of Marketing,* 53, 2 (April), 36-47.

_____ and D. Wayne Norvell (1991), "Personal Characteristics and Salespersons' Justifications as Moderators of Supervisory Discipline in Cases

Involving Unethical Behavior," *Journal of the Academy of Marketing Science,* 19, 1 (Winter), 11-16.

Bingham, Frank G. and Barney T. Raffield, III (1989), "An Overview of Ethical Considerations in Industrial Marketing," in *Developments in Marketing Science, Vol. XII, Proceedings of the Thirteenth Annual Conference of the Academy of Marketing Science,* Jon M. Hawes and John Thanopoulos, eds., Orlando, FL, May 17-20, 244-8.

Browning, Edgar K. and Jacqueline M. Browning (1983), *Microeconomic Theory and Applications,* Boston: Little, Brown.

Burns, David J., and John Brady (1991), "Ethical Perceptions of Future Business Personnel: An Intercultural Perspective," *1991 AMA Winter Educators' Conference,* Chicago: AMA, 411-2.

Chonko, Lawrence, and Shelby D. Hunt (1985), "Ethics and Marketing Management: An Empirical Examination," *Journal of Business Research,* 13 (August), 339-59.

Etzioni, Amitai (1975), *A Comparative Analysis of Complex Organizations,* rev. ed. New York: Free Press.

_____ (1988), *The Moral Dimension: Toward a New Economics,* New York: Free Press.

Ferrell, O. C. and John Fraedrich (1988), "A Descriptive Approach to Understand Ethical Behavior," in *1988 AMA Winter Educators' Conference Marketing: A Return to the Broader Dimensions,* Stanley Shapiro and A. H. Walle, eds., Chicago, IL: American Marketing Association, 194-6.

_____ and Larry G. Gresham (1985), "A Contingency Framework for Understanding Ethical Decision Making in Marketing," *Journal of Marketing,* 49 (Summer), 87-96.

_____ , Larry G. Gresham, and John Fraedrich (1989), "A Synthesis of Ethical Decision Models for Marketing," *Journal of Macromarketing,* (Fall), 55-64.

Frankena, William (1973), *Ethics,* Englewood Cliffs, NJ: Prentice-Hall.

Fried, Charles (1964), "Moral Causation," *Harvard Law Review,* 77 (May), 1258-70.

Harris, C. E., Jr. (1986), *Applying Moral Theories,* Belmont, CA: Wadsworth.

Hite, Robert E., Joseph A. Bellizi, and Cynthia Fraser (1988), "A Content Analysis of Ethical Policy Statements Regarding Marketing Activities," *Journal of Business Ethics,* 10, 7 (October), 771-6.

Hoffman, Martin L. (1983), "Affective and Cognitive Processes in Moral Internalization," in *Social Cognition and Social Development,* E. Tory Higgins, Diane N. Ruble, and Willard W. Hartups, eds., Cambridge: Cambridge University Press.

Hoffman, Elizabeth (1985), "Entitlements, Rights, and Fairness: An Experimental Examination of Subjects' Concepts of Distributive Justice," *Journal of Legal Studies,* 14 (June), 259-97.

Hunt, Shelby D. (1990), "Commentary on an Empirical Investigation of a General Theory of Marketing Ethics," *Journal of the Academy of Marketing Science*, 18, 2 (Spring), 173-7.

_____ (1991), *Modern Marketing Theory: Critical Issues in the Philosophy of Marketing Science*, Cincinnati: South-Western Publishing.

_____, Lawrence B. Chonko, and James B. Wilcox (1984), "Ethical Problems of Marketing Researchers," *Journal of Marketing Research*, 21 (August), 309-324.

_____ and Arturo Z. Vásquez-Párraga (1993), "Organizational Consequences, Marketing Ethics, and Salesforce Supervision," *Journal of Marketing Research*, 30 (February), 78-90.

_____ and Scott Vitell (1986), "A General Theory of Marketing Ethics," *Journal of Macromarketing*, 6, 1 (Spring), 5-16.

Kirk, Roger E. (1982), *Experimental Design: Procedures for the Behavioral Sciences*, Belmont, CA: Brooks/Cole.

Kohlberg, Lawrence (1981), *Essays on Moral Development*, San Francisco: Harper and Row.

Laczniak, Gene R. and Edward J. Inderrieden (1987), "The Influence of Stated Organizational Concern Upon Ethical Decision Making," *Journal of Business Ethics*, 6 (May), 297-307.

McPherson, Michael S. (1984), "Limits on Self-Seeking: The Role of Morality in Economic Life," In *Neoclassical Political Economy*, David C. Colander, ed., Cambridge: University Press.

Murphy, Patrick E. and Gene R. Laczniak (1981), "Marketing Ethics: A Review with Implications for Managers, Educators and Researchers," in *Review of Marketing 1981*, Ben M. Enis and Kenneth J. Roering, eds., Chicago, IL: American Marketing Association, 251-66.

Podsakoff, Philip M. (1982), "Determinants of a Supervisor's Use of Rewards and Punishments: A Literature Review and Suggestions for Further Research," *Organizational Behavior and Human Performance*, 29 (February), 58-83.

Posner, Barry Z. and Warren H. Schmidt (1987), "Ethics in American Companies: A Managerial Perspective," *Journal of Business Ethics*, 6 (July), 383-91.

Ronen, Simcha (1986), *Comparative and Multinational Management*, New York: Wiley.

Ross, William David (1930), *The Right and The Good*, Oxford: Clarendon Press.

Rossi, Peter H., James D. Wright, and Andy B. Anderson (1983), *Handbook of Survey Research*. New York: Academic Press, Inc.

Schein, E.H. (1985), *Organizational Culture and Leadership*, S. Francisco, CA: Jossey-Bass.

Schneider, Benjamin, and A. E. Reichers (1983), "On the Etiology of Climates," *Personnel Psychology*, 36, 19-40.

Schoorman, F. David, and Benjamin Schneider (1988), "Grappling with Work Facilitation: An Evolving Approach to Understanding Work Effectiveness," in *Facilitating Work Effectiveness*, F. David Schoorman, and Benjamin Schneider, eds., Lexington, MA: Lexington Books, 3-20.

Consumer Ethics in Developing Countries: An Empirical Investigation

Jamal A. Al-Khatib
Kathryn Dobie
Scott J. Vitell

SUMMARY. Operating within a global competitive environment poses many problems for American firms. One question receiving only passing attention is how the ethical perceptions of consumers can impact the global operations of the firm. The conflict between domestic and non-domestic ethical norms as to the conduct of business operations has been the subject of governmental scrutiny. However, the impact of differences in consumer ethical norms has not been addressed. Understanding such differences may have relevance for decisions related to the workforce, plant location, and choice of vendors and/or distributors. The current study is designed to investigate the relationship between the consumer's ideology and perceptions of ethical behavior.

The relationship between ethics and business has long been a sticking point for business managers as well as the publics that they serve (Baumhart, 1961). Clarification of the nature of ethical behav-

---

Jamal A. Al-Khatib is Assistant Professor of Marketing at the University of Wisconsin-Eau Claire. Kathryn Dobie is Assistant Professor of Marketing at the University of Wisconsin-Eau Claire. Scott J. Vitell is Associate Professor of Marketing at the University of Mississippi.

[Haworth co-indexing entry note]: "Consumer Ethics in Developing Countries: An Empirical Investigation." Al-Khatib, Jamal A., Kathryn Dobie, and Scott J. Vitell. Co-published simultaneously in the *Journal of Euromarketing* (International Business Press, an imprint of The Haworth Press, Inc.) Vol. 4, No. 2, 1995, pp. 87-109; and: *Ethical Issues in International Marketing* (ed: Nejdet Delener) International Business Press, an imprint of The Haworth Press, Inc., 1995, pp. 87-109. Multiple copies of this article/chapter may be purchased from The Haworth Document Delivery Center [1-800-3-HAWORTH; 9:00 a.m. - 5:00 p.m. (EST)].

87

ior and the application of ethics in the business context have proven to be particularly thorny issues. Bartel's (1967) discourse on ethics emphasized that ethics is peculiar to relationships and activities. Hunt, Chonko, and Wilcox (1984) noted that personal value systems include those obligations which the individual feels toward others. As an individual's ethical or moral philosophy is couched in his/her principles and values, and is based on situational interaction, it is not surprising that Ferrell and Gresham (1985) indicated the general lack of agreement among business leaders as to what constitutes ethical behavior. From a corporate behavior perspective, Hunt, Wood and Chonko (1989) proposed that ". . . corporate ethical values are . . . a composite of the individual ethical values of managers and . . . policies on ethics of the organization" (p. 79).

If businesses are to become more global in nature, an understanding of the ethical norms of different ethnic groups and cultures is requisite for a more complete understanding of the cultural environment in which the firm must operate (Bartels, 1967; Becker and Fritzsche, 1987). Identification of differences between the ethical expectations and behaviors of the host consumer population and the firm could provide insight regarding consumer attitude vis à vis the firm. From a managerial perspective, ethical considerations may potentially affect aspects of firm operations such as worker attitudes and behaviors, common business practices, governmental attitudes, and consumer perceptions of the firm and its product offerings (Vitell, Nwachukwu, and Barnes, 1993; Dolecheck, 1992; Akaah, 1990).

Business managers have come to recognize the importance of differentiating the marketing mix to respond to the more easily discernable elements of different cultural environments. Similarly, differences in consumers' ethical values and practices may influence their attitude toward both firm and product offering. This study proposes that culturally grounded ethical values, in both a personal and business context, are revealed in the relationship between the consumer's ethical ideology and his/her perceptions of ethical behavior.

PREVIOUS RESEARCH

Because ethical issues are so intricately intertwined in a firm's interactions with its various publics, and because of the increased public and regulatory concern regarding the environmental and social effects of business operations, the study of ethical behavior in a business context has assumed a greater level of importance (Hunt and Vitell, 1986, 1992; Ferrell, Gresham and Fraedrich, 1989). This increased concern is reflected in the establishment of academic publications devoted to ethical issues (e.g., *Journal of Business Ethics*), devotion of special issues on the topic, (e.g., *Journal of Euromarketing*), topical conferences, the establishment of endowed positions at academic institutions, and AACSB accreditation standards. Marketing, the boundary position between the firm and its publics, has been the focus of much of the research related to business ethics (Ferrell and Gresham, 1985; Hunt and Vitell, 1986; Ferrell, Gresham, and Fraedrich, 1989; Hunt and Vitell, 1992; Singhapakdi and Vitell, 1993a; Singhapakdi and Vitell, 1993b). This is not surprising, as much of the potential opportunity for unethical behavior exists within the marketing function, particularly at the buyer/seller interface (Vitell and Festervand, 1987). The results of these studies indicate that personal (Singhapakdi and Vitell, 1993a) and professional (Singhapakdi and Vitell, 1993b) values are related to the marketer's moral philosophy and decision making in ethical situations.

To date, the majority of ethics related research has focused on the seller side of the buyer/seller dyad. The relatively few studies which have been concerned with the buyer side of the dyad can be grouped into four general categories. The first group of studies are those which have focused on specific behavioral issues such as shoplifting (Kallis, Krentier, and Vanier, 1986; Moschis and Powell, 1986) and ecologically related consumption (Antil, 1984; Haldeman, Peters, and Tripple, 1987).

A second area of study has focused on understanding the consumer's ethical decision making process. From a conceptual perspective, Grove, Vitell, and Strutton (1989) proposed a model incorporating neutralization to explain the rationalization by consumers of non-normative behavior. An empirical study by Davis (1979) found that consumers were willing to assert their "rights" as outlined in John F. Kennedy's "Consumer Bill of Rights," but they were not willing to accept their corresponding responsibilities. DePaulo (1987) investigated differences in perceptions as to the ethical nature of behaviors based on who performs the action. Results indicated that consumers were more critical of the seller than of the buyer when an unethical action was committed.

The third stream of consumer ethics research focuses on consumer reactions to the ethical behavior of the firm. These reactions hinge on the interaction of consumer perceptions of ethical activity, the actions of the firm, and consumer sensitivity to perceived ethical and unethical actions. Therefore, a lack of information regarding consumer ethical beliefs could contribute to an incomplete understanding of the ethical issues facing the firm. Research concerning consumer perceptions of ethical behavior has revealed that consumers not only judge actions to be "wrong," but that there is also a "grey" area in which the judgement of wrongness was based on the identity of the perpetrator of the action (Wilkes, 1978). Unlike the results of the DePaulo (1987) study, the latitude of tolerance revealed in the Wilkes study was directed toward business actions as opposed to the actions of the consumer. More recent work in the area has tried to identify whether various demographic factors influence what actions are perceived to be unethical (Vitell, Lumpkin, and Rawwas, 1991; Muncy and Vitell, 1992). The major drawbacks of these studies are the use of limited samples (e.g., students and the elderly), and the narrow breadth of issues addressed.

The final aspect of ethics related research, thus far receiving only summary attention, relates to the increased globalization of business (Bartels, 1967). While the influence of culture vis à vis the marketing mix has been readily acknowledged, few studies have addressed culturally related ethical issues (Becker and Fritzsche, 1987; Akaah, 1990; Vitell, Nwachukwu and Barnes, 1993). Further studies conducted at the consumer level are needed to provide information regarding differences in ethical practices, and to determine the compatibility of firm and culture ethical behavior.

THE STUDY

The current study is intended as an exploratory investigation into the relationship between the consumer's espoused ideology and his/her perception of ethical behavior. The specific research question to be addressed is the following:

Is the consumer's choice of action in an ethics related situation explained by his/her ethical orientation?

The ethical orientation of the consumer will be determined using three independent constructs, Machiavellianism, Relativism, and Idealism. The Machiavellianism construct is designed to measure the individual's general strategy for dealing with others. This construct measures the degree to which the individual feels that others are manipulative in interpersonal situations. The Relativism construct measures the degree to which the individual's ethical behavior reflects universal or absolute moral principles. Idealism measures the degree to which the consumer believes that the "right" action will produce the desired consequences (Forsyth, 1980). The relativism and idealism constructs provide the deontological and teleological underpinnings of an individual's ethical behavior (Hunt and Vitell, 1986).

The Research Setting

The present study's setting was Cairo, Egypt. Egypt is a developing country that has assumed a strategically significant political and economic role in the Middle Eastern region. With a population of fifty-four million, it is the most heavily populated Arab state, and the second most populous country on the African continent. Ninety-nine percent of the population resides in urban areas (The World Fact Book, 1991).

The economic impact of Egypt's public and private sectors should not be underestimated. It has one of the largest public sectors of all third world economies. Average annual growth in general government consumption was 5.3 percent between 1980 and 1987. Private consumption grew at an annual rate of 5 percent during this same time period (El-Naggar, 1990). Because of this rate of growth in both the private and public sectors, Egypt has become an important market for many American, European, and Japanese firms. The estimated value of exports to Egypt from the U.S., E.C., Japan and Eastern Europe totaled $3.8 billion in 1989.

Egyptians have been receptive to joint investment and business opportunities. Out of the total of 7.3 billion Egyptian pounds (EP 2.90 = US $1, January 1, 1992) invested in Egypt up to mid-1987, foreign investment accounted for 35 percent of the total: the Arab oil-exporting states 18 percent, the U. S. 5.3 percent, the European Community 6.1 percent, and 5.6 percent from all other nations. The remaining investment, 65 percent, was contributed by Egyptians (Oweiss, 1990, p. 26-27).

Egypt has a strong domestic economic position with a Total Gross Domestic Product (GDP) of $37 billion. Per capita income is $700, putting Egypt in the middle range of all developing countries on this measure. These economic measures indicate the presence of a large potential market. An additional encouraging factor for foreign investors is that the Egyptian consumer has demonstrated a receptivity to Western products (Rice and Mahmoud, 1985).

The combination of a large potential consumer market, receptivity to Western products, and positive attitude toward foreign investment by the Egyptian business community serves to position Egypt as not only a large potential consumer market but also as a base for serving the Middle Eastern region (Foreign Economic Trends, 1991).

Cairo, with a population of approximately 9 million, is the largest city in Egypt. Being the capital, and the political and economic center of the country, its population is composed of long-time urban dwellers as well as rural migrants who have come to the city for employment opportunities. Even more important, from a marketing perspective, is the generally high level of receptivity vis à vis Western products and marketing practices, i.e., marketing research. The cosmopolitan orientation of Cairo combined with a generally higher level of education, receptivity to imported products, and income of the population defines the probable target market of most non-national corporations.

The Sample

The lack of sampling resources and the obstacles encountered when sampling a poor, mobile and illiterate population prevented the sampling of large segments of the Egyptian population. This forced the researchers to abandon more precise sampling techniques, i.e., probability samples, in favor of the more realistically obtained convenience sample (Kaynak, 1978; Dant and Barnes, 1988; Tuncalp, 1988; Tuncalp and Yavas, 1983; Yavas and Kaynak, 1980). The convenience sample consisted of 500 consumers living in Cairo, Egypt during the summer of 1990. The test instrument was hand delivered due to the lack of a reliable postal service. Ten days after delivery, the test instrument was hand collected (Tuncalp, 1988). There were 348 returned responses of which 318 were usable, giving a response rate of 63.6%. The sample utilized in the study consisted of 40% married, 58% male, and 67% with a college degree.

The present study's sample was skewed in favor of educated and professional consumers. Despite the lack of proportionate representation by less educated segments of the Egyptian market, the researchers considered the sample to be appropriate. The rationale for this decision was based on factors which characterize lower socioeconomic classes in developing countries:

1. the absence of opinion formation among lower classes and their subsequent difficulty in expressing opinion.
2. the negative attitude toward and lack of appreciation for marketing research.
3. the inherent greater bias associated with respondents facing economic hardship relative to that faced by the more educated and well-to-do respondent, particularly when the issue under investigation (i.e., consumption ethic) is highly sensitive to social and economic conditions of the respondents.
4. the prohibitive cost of reaching poorer areas and respondents with low education levels.
5. the general mistrust of strangers which tends to obstruct the conducting of survey research. The level of mistrust tends to have an inverse relationship to the respondent's social and economic class (Kaynak, 1978; Tuncalp and Yavas, 1983; Yavas and Kaynak, 1980).

Independent Variables

The independent variables used in this study, Machiavellianism, Relativism, and Idealism, are designed to reflect the consumer's ideological mindset. Use of these established constructs provides a commonality with previous ethics related research (Muncy and Vitell, 1989; Al-Khatib, Vitell and Rawwas, 1994; Rawwas, Vitell and Al-Khatib, 1994; Vitell, Lumpkin and Rawwas, 1991).

The Machiavellianism construct was measured using the MACH IV scale of Christie and Geis (1970). There are twenty items evenly divided between Machiavellian and non-Machiavellian intent (see Appendix I) in this scale. The respondents indicated agreement or disagreement with the twenty statements using a five-point Likert scale. The Cronbach's Alpha of 0.574 indicates a scale reliability which is comparable to the 0.76 obtained by Hunt and Chonko (1984) and the split-half reliability of 0.79 obtained by Christie and Geis (1970). The difference in Cronbach Alpha is due to the translation and application of scales that have been written in one language (i.e., English) and translated and applied in another language and culture (i.e., Arabic) (Brislin, 1970; Mitchell, 1966; Dant and Barnes, 1988; David, Douglas and Silk, 1981). For example, Mitchell (1966), in assessing the impact of the quality of survey's translation on statement reliability, found that translated statements or questions highest in rated clarity were highest in reliability.

The Ethics Position Questionnaire (see Appendix II) developed by Forsyth (1980) was used to measure the predominant ethical perspective of the respondents. This instrument consists of two 10 item scales. One measures the level of idealism, the acceptance of moral absolutes. The second measures relativism, the rejection of universal moral principles. Agreement or disagreement with the statements was indicated using a 5-point Likert-type scale. Cronbach's Alpha for the Idealism scale was 0.763, and for the Relativism scale 0.787.

In order to verify the separateness of the independent variables, correlations between the three constructs were checked. The correlation between Machiavellianism and Idealism was − .3132, while the correlation between Machiavellianism and Relativism is .3945. Idealism and Relativism had a correlation of − .1721. The level of correlation is well below that which would be expected if there was a relationship between the three constructs, indicating that Machiavellianism, Relativism, and Idealism are separate constructs.

Dependent Variables

The dependent variables are derived from the "consumer ethics" scale (see Appendix III) developed by Muncy and Vitell (1989) and validated by Vitell, Lumpkin, and Rawwas (1991). This scale is designed to measure one's beliefs regarding twenty consumer situations which have ethical implications. There are four dimensions to this construct, each of which is used as a dependent variable in this study. The first dimension, *Actively Benefiting from Illegal Activity (CE1)*, deals with actions initiated by the consumer, and are likely to be considered illegal by most consumers. The second dimension, *Passively Benefiting (CE2)*, involves instances where the consumer stands to benefit from the seller's mistake and does not inform the seller or correct the situation. However, the consumer does not initiate these actions. The third dimension, *Actively Benefiting from Questionable Action (CE3)*, involves self-initiated actions that are questionable but are not illegal. The fourth and final dimension, *No harm/no foul (CE4)*, involves actions in which little or no harm results and is perceived by some consumers to be acceptable (Table 1).

TABLE 1. Reliability of Constructs.

Variables	Number of Statements	Cronbach Alpha
Actively benefiting from illegal activity CE1	4	.7237
Passively benefiting CE2	3	.6969
Actively benefiting from questionable action CE3	1	--
No harm/no foul CE4	3	.4739
Machiavellianism	19	.5749
Relativism	9	.7873
Idealism	10	.7635

The use of dependent and independent variables developed and tested in one culture, and applied in an alternative culture has the potential for losing the emic, or meaningful aspects, of the other culture. It has been noted that to ensure reliability and validity in the cross-cultural application of a research instrument, the use of a standardized instrument should be avoided (Brislin, Lonner and Thorndike, 1973). To address this potential problem, a five-step guideline for applying a domestically developed instrument in alternate cultures proposed by Dant and Barnes (1988) was utilized as follows:

1. determining whether the construct has the same exact meaning in the alternative culture.
2. determining whether the construct has a different meaning in the alternative culture.
3. determining whether the construct indicators have no meaning in the alternative culture.
4. determining whether the construct indicators have a different meaning in the alternative culture.
5. determining whether the indicators can be directly measured.

The test instrument was examined to determine whether any of these five concerns was a factor in the present study. Consequently, the following actions were taken:

1. eliminating items from the original instrument due to lack of meaning in the Egyptian culture (e.g., CE2 item #4 or MECH 17).
2. ensuring that the indicators had the same meaning through the use of the back translation technique (Brislin, 1970).
3. examining auxiliary theories implicit in the choice of indicators in the original instrument to ensure that indicators selected for the Egyptian version of the instrument would have the same emic meaning as in the original instrument.
4. training interviewers to stress the academic nature of the project, and the absence of any right or wrong answer to any of the questions in the survey. This was crucial because in the Egyptian culture the "saving of face" is an emic imperative and

complicates the collection of data regarding socially sensitive issues.

Results of the Study

Four regression equations were used to determine the relationship between the consumer's perceptions of ethical behavior and their basic ideological philosophy (Table 2).

The first equation addressed situations in which the action would be considered by most consumers to be illegal. The ideological variables explained 33% of the variance in the dependent variable (CE1). Idealism is the most influential variable in this equation (Beta = $-.519$, significant at $p < .01$). The direction of the sign indicates an inverse relationship between an idealistic ethical philosophy and engaging in illegal activity. Conversely, as indicated by the sign, consumers ascribing to a relativistic ethical ideology would be more likely to initiate an illegal activity from which they would benefit (Beta = .161, significant at $p < .01$). Since Machiavellian characteristics measure perceptions of treatment by others, it is not surprising that this construct was not a significant factor in the first set of equations.

In the second equation, the consumer stands to benefit from the seller's mistake and does not inform the seller or correct the situation (CE2). In this scenario, the consumer's ideology explained 32% of the variance in the response to the presented ethical situations ($R^2 = .327$). Those ascribing to an idealistic ideology were most prone to find situations in which the consumer might benefit at the expense of others to be unacceptable (Beta = $-.518$, significant at $p < .01$). Those ascribing to a relativistic ideology would be more likely to find those same situations acceptable (Beta = .140, significant at $p < .01$). Machiavellian tendencies did not contribute to the explanatory power of this equation.

In situations in which an individual would actively benefit as a result of an action that is questionable but not illegal (CE3), the role of personal ideology is not as clearcut. Ideological orientation explains little of the variance in the dependent variable ($R^2 = .07$). For these models, the Machiavellianism construct assumes the greatest role in explaining the variance in consumer actions (Beta = .205, significant at $p < .01$). As a measure of consumer's percep-

TABLE 2. Regression Analysis Results.

Dependent Variable	Independent Variables			R²	F
	Relativism	Idealism	Machiavellianism		
Actively benefiting from illegal activity CE1	.161*	−.519*	.024	.334	52.87*
Passively benefiting CE2	.140*	−.518*	.032	.327	51.14*
Actively benefiting from questionable action CE3	−.022	−.134**	.205*	.073	8.31*
No harm/no foul CE4	.081	−.035	.139**	.040	4.40*

*   Significant at p < .01
** Significant at p < .05

tions of their treatment by others, the strength of this construct may indicate that responses to questionable actions might hinge on situational factors, (e.g., intent), as opposed to absolute ethical values. This proposition is given additional support by the relative lack of explanatory power of the Idealism construct, and the lack of significance of the Relativism construct.

When investigating those situations in which it is perceived that no harm is done (CE4), the explanatory power of the model drops precipitously ($R^2 = .04$). The only significant independent variable is the Machiavellianism construct (Beta = .139, significant at $p < .05$). This seems to imply that in situations where there is no clear intent to do harm or take advantage of others, situational factors take precedence over absolute ethical codes of conduct.

DISCUSSION

The results of this study provide thought-provoking insights regarding the research question which provided the impetus for this study.

> Is a consumer's choice of action in an ethics related situation explained by his/her ethical orientation?

The strength of the idealistic and relativistic personal ideologies as explanatory variables in cases in which the activity in question is either illegal or is clearly detrimental to another indicates that in more clear-cut situations, personal ideology influences perceptions of the "rightness" or "wrongness" of the action in question. As might be expected, those consumers having an idealistic ethical ideology are less likely to engage in activities judged to be illegal or take advantage of others than are those with a relativistic ethical ideology.

However, in situations in which the activities in question either are not illegal, even though some may judge them to be unethical, or cause no immediately discernable harm, the predominant explanatory variable is the Machiavellianism construct. This leads to the supposition that when the "right" and "wrong" are not clearcut, situational factors dominate consumer's judgements as to the appropriateness of the activity.

From these observations, several initial guidelines for managerial action can be drawn. First, if the consumer's personal ideology affects perceptions of ethical activity only in those situations where the action is contrary to law or causes obvious harm to another, then, the legal code and the ideological frame of the consumer must be considered when assessing the possibility of firm/consumer ethical conflict.

Secondly, it is necessary to determine what actions fall into the "grey" area where attribution as to intent or consequences determines the consumer's likelihood of condoning or engaging in that action. Perceptions as to the appropriateness of a given behavior under these circumstances is likely to be influenced by situational factors such as religion, education, and the political and economic climate.

Managerial Implications

As the results of this initial exploratory research effort suggest, a knowledge of the consumer's ethical ideology should assist managers as they attempt to determine the probable actions of consumers only when there are clearly defined legal mandates or when harm to others may result. This suggests that, contrary to the findings of Becker and Fritzsche (1987), an understanding of the ethical norms of countries in which multinational firms market and conduct operations is not sufficient to avoid conflicts between the firm and its multicultural publics. Therefore, as this research suggests, managers would be well-advised to codify the desirable and undesirable behavioral activities of host-country office staff, workers, customers, and suppliers. The firm's ethical code, structure, and procedures must also be clearly defined. These actions would reduce the scope of "grey" areas which would be vulnerable to interpretation according to individual perceptions of intent or harm. In addition to codifying the expected behaviors of both firm and publics, where appropriate, contractual procedures can be instituted to ensure adherence to the proscribed codes of conduct. The intent of these actions is to promote a smoother working relationship between firm and publics by reducing the number of situations in which the appropriate action is not apparent.

These actions serve to cultivate an appreciation of the ethical position of the firm. Additional methods of cultivating adherence to the ethical position of the firm might include efforts which serve to remind the various publics of the firm that their actions directly and indirectly impact the welfare of others through their spiritual, cultural and religious hopes, dreams, ideals and inspirations. Advertising can be designed to emphasize these virtues and direct the behavior of consumers towards veracity and integrity. Well-executed promotion may have a significant impact on controlling problems linked to ethical behavior and alleviating some of their consequences.

The burden of responsibility for demonstrating the desired ethical behaviors rests on the management and employees of the firm. They serve as role models, demonstrating the desired societal behaviors. In fact, consumers do tend to emulate marketers when they are in the marketplace. An honest advertisement and a quality product can create a virtuous environment which might result in more trustworthy exchanges between marketers and consumers.

Limitations of the Study

One area of concern which may influence the findings of this study relates to the political, economic and religious state of the country. Care should be taken when interpreting the findings of the study to consider such factors upon the individual's perceptions of the importance of ethical behavior. As previous studies suggest (Rawwas, Vitell and Al-Khatib, 1994; Al-Khatib, Vitell, and Rawwas, 1994), political instability or civil unrest and economic hardship may cause tense, pessimistic, and struggling individuals to sacrifice ethicality for basic survival needs. Similarly, the religious influence on the individual may play a factor in their perception of "right and wrong" behaviors. Egypt is largely a Muslim country which in recent years has experienced an increased Fundamentalist Islamic movement. The Fundamentalist movement advocates an idealistic approach to life which might result in the adoption of a double ethical standard by the Egyptian consumer. One standard is used to handle daily decisions while another, influenced by their religion's teaching, is not implementable because of the economic hardships faced by the population.

Courtesy bias, a well-documented problem faced when conducting research in developing countries, may have been a factor in this study. It is possible that the hand delivery and pick-up of the research instrument may have motivated respondents to provide the most socially acceptable answers (Akaah, 1990).

Because of the composition of the sample, the results of this study should be interpreted with the understanding that the sample is only representative of the educated portion of the population. However, this population, while being arithmetically small, is an economically powerful portion of the Egyptian market (Oweiss, 1990).

Directions for Future Research

Suggestions for future research center on discovery of the commonality of ethical behavior. Research efforts directed toward:

1. discovering those factors which most influence the ethical behavior of consumers, and
2. differentiating between situational/environmental factors and ideological factors,

would assist managers as they develop strategies and policies relative to all the publics of the firm.

The first step in the discovery of ethical commonalities is dependent upon the development of a scale which provides a valid and reliable cross cultural measurement of personal ideological philosophy. Such a measure would facilitate the comparability of studies.

The second area of study would involve the inclusion of situational and cultural variables as possible determinants of ethical behavior. This knowledge could provide valuable input for planning and designing corporate and consumer contact environments such that ethical behavior is encouraged.

The thrust of future research efforts should not be confined to the identification of ideological norms in different cultural settings. Instead the intent should be to identify not only the individual's ethical orientation but also those factors which influence his/her perceptions of ethical behaviors. This knowledge will aid managers in their efforts to develop a compatible relationship with the publics that they serve.

AUTHOR NOTES

Jamal A. Al-Khatib holds a PhD from the University of Mississippi.
Kathryn Dobie holds a PhD from Memphis State University.
Scott J. Vitell holds the Starnes Lectureship in Marketing and Business Ethics at the University of Mississippi.

REFERENCES

Akaah, Ishmael P. (1990). Attitudes of marketing professionals toward ethics in marketing research: A cross-national comparison. *Journal of Business Ethics, 9*, 45-53.

Al-Khatib J., Vitell, S. & Rawwas, M. (1994). Consumer ethics: A cross cultural investigation. In *Advances in International Marketing*, Cavusgil, T., ed.

Antil, J. H. (1984). Socially responsible consumers: Profile and implications for public policy. *Journal of Macromarketing, 4*, 18-39.

Bartels, R. (1967). A model for ethics in marketing. *Journal of Marketing, 31*, 20-26.

Baumhart, R. C. (1961). How ethical are businessmen? *Harvard Business Review, 39*, 6-19, 156-76.

Becker, H. & Fritzsche, D. J. (1987). A comparison of the ethical behavior of American, French, and German managers. *Columbia Journal of World Business*, 87-95.

Brislin, R. W. (1970). Back translation for cross-cultural research. *Journal of Cross-Cultural Psychology, 1*, 185-216.

_____, Lonner, W. & Thorndike, R. (1973). *Cross-Cultural Research Methods*. New York: John Wiley.

Christie, R. & Geis, F. L. (1970). *Studies in Machiavellianism*. New York: Academic Press.

Dant, R. P. & Barnes, J. H. (1988). Methodological concerns in cross-cultural research: Implications for economic development. *Research in Marketing, Supplement 4, Marketing and Development: Toward Broader Dimensions*. JAI Press, 149-171.

Davis, H. L., Douglas, S. P. & Silk, A. J. (1981). Measure unreliability: A hidden threat to cross-cultural marketing research? *Journal of Marketing, 45*, 98-109.

Davis, R. M. (1979). Comparison of consumer acceptance of rights and responsibilities. In *Ethics and the Consumer Interest*. N. M. Ackerman, ed., 68-70.

DePaulo, P. J. (1986). Ethical perceptions of deceptive bargaining tactics used by salespersons and customers: A double standard. In Proceedings of the Division of Consumer Psychology. Joel G. Sagert, ed., American Psychological Association, Washington, D. C.

Dolecheck, M. M. (1992). Cross-cultural analysis of business ethics: Hong Kong and American business personnel. *Journal of Managerial Issues, 4*, 288-303.

El-Naggar, F. R. (1980). Middle eastern business intensity and market growth (1970-1980): An overview. *Journal of Contemporary Business, 9*(3), 71-84.

Ferrell, O. C. & Gresham, L. (1985). A contingency framework for understanding ethical decision making in marketing. *Journal of Marketing*, (Summer), 87-96.

_____, _____, & Fraedrich, J. (1989). A synthesis of ethical decision models for marketing. *Journal of Macromarketing*, (Fall), 55-64.

Foreign Economic Trends (1992). Office of the United States Trade Representative, 61-65.

Forsyth, D. R. (1980). A taxonomy of ethical ideologies. *Journal of Personality and Social Psychology, 39*(1), 175-84.

Grove, S. J., Vitell, S. J. & Strutton, D. (1989). Non-normative consumer behavior and the techniques of neutralization. In Proceedings of the 1989 AMA Winter Educator's Conference, ed. Richard Bagozzi and J. Paul Peter, Chicago, IL: American Marketing Association, 131-5.

Haldeman, V. A., Peters, J. M. & Trippel, P. A. (1987). Measuring a consumer energy conservation ethic: An analysis of components. *Journal of Consumer Affairs, 21*(1), 70-85.

Hunt, S. D. & Chonko, L. (1984). Marketing and Machiavellianism. *Journal of Marketing*, (Summer), 30-42.

_____, & Wilcox, J. B. (1984). Ethical problems of marketing researchers. *Journal of Marketing Research, 21*, 309-24.

_____, Wood, V. R. & Chonko, L. (1989). Corporate ethical values and organizational commitment in marketing. *Journal of Marketing, 53*, 79-90.

_____ & Vitell, S. J. (1986). A general theory of marketing ethics. *Journal of Macromarketing*, (Spring), 5-16.

_____&_____ (1992). The general theory of marketing ethics: A retrospective and revision. In *Ethics in Marketing*, eds. Quelch and Smith, Richard D. Irwin: Chicago.

Kallis, M. J., Krentier, K. A. & Vanier, D. J. (1986). The value of user image in quelling aberrant consumer behavior. *Journal of the Academy of Marketing Science, 14*, 29-35.

Kaynak, E. (1978). Difficulties of undertaking marketing research in the developing countries. *European Research*, November, 251-259.

Mayer, C. S. (1978). Multinational marketing research: The magnifying glass of methodological problems. *European Research*, March, 77-84.

Mitchell, R. (1966). Survey materials collected in the developing countries: sampling, measurement, and interviewing obstacles to intra and international comparisons. *International Social Science Journal, 17*, 665-6.

Moschis, G. P. & Powell, J. (1986). The juvenile shoplifter. *The Marketing Mix, 10*(1), 1.

Muncy, J. A. & Vitell, S. J. (1989). Consumer ethics: An empirical investigation of the ethical beliefs of the final consumer. *Journal of Business Research*, forthcoming.

Oweiss, I. M. (1990). Egypt's economy: The pressing issues. In I.M. Oweiss (ed.), *Political Economy of Contemporary Egypt*, (pp. 3-49), Georgetown University Press.

Rawwas, M., Vitell, S. & Al-Khatib, J. (1994). The impact of terrorism and civil unrest on consumer ethics. *Journal of Business Ethics*, 13.

Rice, G. & Mahmoud, E. (1985). The prospects for export marketing to Egypt. In E. Kaynak (Ed.), *International Business in the Middle East*, 217-228.

Singhapakdi, A. & Vitell, S. J. (1993a). Personal values underlying the moral philosophies of marketing professionals. *Business & Professional Ethics Journal, 12*(1), 1-16.

_____(1993b). Personal and professional values underlying the ethical judgements of marketers. *Journal of Business Ethics, 12*, 65-73.

The World Fact Book, (1991). Central Intelligence Agency, Public Affairs, 89-90.

Tuncalp, S. (1988). *The Marketing Research Scene in Saudi Arabia*, College of Industrial Management, University of Petroleum and Minerals, Dhahran, Saudi Arabia.

_____ & Yavas, U. (1983). Supermarkets gaining rapid acceptance in Saudi Arabia. *Marketing News*, (February 4), 5.

Vitell, S. J. & Festervand, T. (1987). Business ethics: Conflicts, practices and beliefs of industrial executives. *Journal of Business Ethics, 6*, 111-222.

_____, Lumpkin, J. R. & Rawwas, M. (1991). Consumer ethics: An investigation of the ethical beliefs of elderly consumers. *Journal of Business Ethics*, (May), 365-375.

Vitell, S. J., Nwachukwu, S. L. & Barnes, J. H. (1993). The effects of culture on ethical decision-making: An application of Hofstede's typology. *Journal of Business Ethics, 12*, 1-18.

Wilkes, R. E. (1978). Fraudulent behavior by consumers. *Journal of Marketing*, (October), 67-75.

Yavas, U. and Kaynak, E. (1980). Current status of marketing research, In "Developing Countries: Problems and Opportunities," *Journal of International Marketing and Marketing Research, 5*(2), 79-89.

APPENDIX I

Machiavellianism Scale

1. Never tell anyone the real reason you did something unless it is useful to do so.
2. The best way to handle people is to tell them what they want to hear.
3. One should take action only when sure it is morally right.
4. Most people are basically good and kind.
5. It is safest to assume that all people have a vicious streak and it will come out when given the chance.
6. Honesty is the best policy in all cases.
7. There is no excuse for lying to someone else.
8. Generally speaking, people won't work hard unless they're forced to do so.
9. All in all, it is better to be humble and honest than to be important and dishonest.
10. When you ask someone to do something for you, it is best to give the real reasons for wanting it rather than giving reasons which carry more weight.
11. People who get ahead in the world live clean, moral lives.
12. Anyone who completely trusts others is asking for big trouble.
13. The biggest difference between criminals and others is that the criminals are stupid enough to get caught.
14. Most people are brave.
15. It is wise to flatter important people.
16. It is possible to be good in all respects.
17. Barnum was wrong when he said that "there's a sucker born every minute."*
18. It is hard to get ahead without cutting corners.
19. People suffering from incurable diseases should have the choice of being painlessly put to death.
20. Most people forget more easily the death of their father than the loss of their property.

* not used due to inapplicability to Egyptian culture

APPENDIX II

Ethics Position Questionnaire

Idealism Scale

1. A person should make certain that their actions never intentionally harm another even to a small degree.
2. Risks to another should never be tolerated, irrespective of how small the risks might be.
3. The existence of potential harm to others is always wrong, irrespective of the benefits to be gained.
4. One should never psychologically or physically harm another.
5. One should not perform an action which might in any way threaten the dignity and welfare of another individual.
6. If an action could harm an innocent other, then it should not be done.
7. Deciding whether or not to perform an act by balancing the positive consequences of the act against the negative consequences of the act is immoral.
8. The dignity and welfare of the people should be the most important concern in any society.
9. It is never necessary to sacrifice the welfare of others.
10. Moral actions are those which closely match the ideals of the most "perfect" action.

Relativism Scale

1. There are no ethical principles that are so important that they should be a part of any code of ethics.
2. What is ethical varies from one situation and society to another.
3. Moral standards should be seen as being individualistic; what one person considers to be moral may be judged to be immoral by another person.
4. Different types of moralities cannot be compared as to "rightness."*
5. What is ethical for everyone can never be resolved since what is moral or immoral is up to the individual.
6. Moral standards are simply personal rules which indicate how a person should behave, and are not to be applied in making judgements of others.
7. Ethical considerations in interpersonal relations are so complex that individuals should be allowed to formulate their own individual codes.

8. Rigidly codifying an ethical position that prevents certain types of actions stands in the way of better human relations and adjustment.
9. No rule concerning lying can be formulated; whether a lie is permissible or not permissible totally depends upon the situation.
10. Whether a lie is judged to be moral or immoral depends upon the circumstances surrounding the action.

* not used due to inapplicability to Egyptian culture

APPENDIX III

Consumer Ethics Scale

Actively benefiting from illegal activity (CE1)

1. Drinking a can of soda in a supermarket without paying for it.
2. Using a long distance code that does not belong to you.*
3. Giving misleading price information to a clerk for an unpriced item.
4. Reporting a lost item as "stolen" to an insurance company in order to collect the money.
5. Changing price-tags on merchandise in a retail store.

Passively benefiting (CE2)

1. Not saying anything when the waitress miscalculates the bill in your favor.
2. Getting too much change and not saying anything.
3. Lying about a child's age in order to get a lower price.
4. Moving into a new residence and finding that the cable TV is still hooked up, and using it rather than signing up and paying for it.*

Actively benefiting from questionable action (CE3)

1. Stretching the truth on an income tax return.*
2. Using a coupon for merchandise you did not buy.*
3. Using an expired coupon for merchandise.*
4. Not telling the truth when negotiating the price of a new automobile.

No harm/no foul (CE4)

1. Taping a movie off the television.
2. Returning merchandise after trying it and not liking it.*

3. Recording an album instead of buying it.
4. Using computer software or games that you did not buy.
5. Spending over an hour trying on different dresses and not purchasing any.

*   not used due to inapplicability to Egyptian culture

Index